OUTWARD BOUND

Ian M. Malcolm

Published in 2017 by
Moira Brown
Broughty Ferry
Dundee. DD5 2HZ
www.publishkindlebooks4u.co.uk

Outward Bound was first published
as a kindle book in 2013.

Copyright © Ian M. Malcolm

The right of Ian M. Malcolm to be identified as the Author
of this work has been asserted in accordance with the
Copyrights, Designs and Patents Act 1988.

All rights reserved. No part of this book may be reprinted or reproduced or utilised in any form or by any electronic, mechanical or other means, now known or hereafter invented, including photocopying or recording, or any information storage or retrieval system, without the permission in writing from the Publisher.

ISBN 978-1-5212-0062-9

1	ANXIETY FOLLOWED BY SUCCESS	1
2	REINSTATEMENT	3
3	HAMBURG	6
4	ANTWERP	10
5	IMMINGHAM AND LONDON	13
6	PROMOTION	16
7	SHIPMATES	18
8	THE PASSAGE TO PIRAEUS	23
9	PIRAEUS/ATHENS AND A REUNION	28
10	GENOA	32
11	ENROUTE TO SOUTH AFRICA	35
12	DURBAN, NATAL	42
13	PORT SAID VIA ADEN	49
14	RETURN TO GENOA	53
15	SECOND VISIT TO DURBAN	56
16	LOURENCO MARQUES	76
17	THE ADOPTION OF THE SAMNESSE	78
18	MASSAWA	84
19	DJIBOUTI VIA ADEN	88
20	BACK TO LOURENCO MARQUES	95
21	DAR ES SALAAM	98
22	CHRISTMAS IN TANGA	100
23	THIRD VISIT TO DURBAN	105
24	PORT SAID VIA ADEN (AGAIN)	109
25	ENROUTE TO VENICE	115

26	VENICE	118
27	TRIPOLI	122
28	BONE AND THE 'LAST LEG'	125
29	LEITH NAUTICAL COLLEGE	130

1   ANXIETY FOLLOWED BY SUCCESS

When I arrived home in Dundee, on 7 October, 1945 after a 10-month voyage on the *Samforth*, I knew that I had to obtain a 2nd Class PMG (Postmaster General's Certificate of Proficiency in Radiotelegraphy) if I were to remain a radio officer in the Merchant Navy. Now that the war was over, the Special Certificate, which I and thousands of others held, was no longer to be a qualification for service on ships large enough to come under the Merchant Shipping (Wireless Telegraphy) Act 1919 and the Merchant Shipping (Safety and Load Line Conventions) Act, 1932. In order to give all ships time to return to the UK, the Special Certificate remained valid on vessels within the scope of these Acts, virtually all the ships of the Merchant Service, until 31 December, 1946, but, henceforth, it was a qualification to serve only on trawlers and other small vessels.

I sat the exam during my leave, but, having failed, anticipated a letter of dismissal from my employer, Alfred Holt & Co., owners of the Blue Funnel Line and the Glen Line. But when a reply-paid telegram arrive on 16 November saying, "REPORT OFFICE NINE AM TUESDAY READY DUTY ACKNOWLEDGE = ODYSSEY", I believed I was to have one more voyage on my Special ticket and travelled to Liverpool with all my seagoing gear. I turned out, however, that Holts called me to Liverpool only to dismiss me and their incorrectly worded telegram cost me the loss of my luggage, as it was stolen from the guard's van on the journey south.

On returning to Dundee, I felt so despondent and sorry for myself that my mother eventually got fed up with my moaning and told me that this was nothing when compared to the indignities which my father had suffered during the Depression of the Thirties. This was the shock I needed. I knew that she was right and that the way forward was to get that 2nd Class PMG.

Most of the students at the Wireless College were in the same position as myself, but there were a few young men wanting to go to sea for the first time and some Polish soldiers, both men and women, studying to acquire some technical knowledge in order to gain employment in this country. And, when some of the Special Certificate students, some of whom never did succeed in passing the 2nd Class exam, made a 'success and failure' table on a spare blackboard, my name was, with hilarity, entered in the failure column.

Due to my abortive studies, I hadn't enjoyed much of a leave, but, now that the pressure of time was removed, enjoyed myself more. And believing that I would return to my old job as a clerk in A & S Henry's jute office when my demob number came up, visited the Office.

I had reported the theft of my luggage to the London Midland & Scottish Railway Company (known as the LMS) and two railway detectives came up to the house to question me about it. They never did find out anything about the theft, but I was asked to complete a form and submit a list of what I had lost in order to obtain compensation. I found this a difficult task and months later would suddenly think of something I had forgotten to put down; usually when I was looking for the thing in question.

Special Certificate candidates, were exempted from the Morse, regulations, and practical tests for the 2nd Class so that they sat only the written paper. They had to make their own exam arrangements with the Postmaster General and on the morning of Friday, 22 February, I was again the sole candidate sitting the exam at the GPO Ship Radio Inspection Office at the entrance to Leith docks. And, having acquired more knowledge, knew that this time I had done reasonably well.

I was anxiously awaiting every post for the result of the examination, when, on the morning of Wednesday 6 March, a relative brought the distressing news that my Uncle Jim had been badly injured by machinery on a farm in the Carse of Gowrie. My mother rushed off to be with her sister at Dundee Royal Infirmary and I was in the house by myself when the second post arrived and I had got my certificate. When my mother returned in tears some hours later with the news that Uncle Jim had died, I didn't know whether to laugh or cry.

2   REINSTATEMENT

Radio officers with 1st and 2nd Class certificates were now in short supply and I could have applied to one of the wireless companies which supplied most shipping companies with both men and equipment. The principal one was Marconi, but others were IMR (International Marine Radio), which supplied Cunard, and Siemens. I believed, however, that being directly employed by a shipping company was preferable to being an outsider placed on board by a wireless company and, besides Holts, Salvesen, Union Castle, Brocklebank and the New Zealand Shipping Company directly employed their radio staff. I gave some consideration about applying to Salvesen as the adventure of whaling in the Antarctic appealed to me, but, in the end, decided on the principle of the 'devil you know' and applied to Holts. They reinstated me and I was told to join the *Samnesse*, in Tilbury, on Monday, 18th March, 1946.

As I had lost all my clothes apart from my No.1 uniform, clothing was now a problem as clothes were still rationed and could not be bought without coupons. I calculated that I required 232 coupons to replace what I had lost, but the Superintendent of the Mercantile Marine Office was permitted to give me only 50 unless the LMS provided me with a 'certificate of loss' which they refused to do until a cash settlement was reached. I bought some whites from a chap who was not returning to sea and dug out an old blue suit which I had discarded when I was 17 and was now too small for me. But the problem of clothes was, nevertheless, a minor one. I was returning to sea as a 'regular' in the Merchant Service, had a second wavy gold band and medal ribbons sewn on my uniform jacket, and, on Monday 18 March, boarded the 8.09pm, overnight, train to London.

When the train arrived in Kings Cross Station, I changed onto a train of the Underground system which, after a brief spell underground, completed the journey, to Tilbury, on the surface. The train was full of Forces personnel travelling to the Continent and, on the way, we stopped at a station where a loudspeaker blared out that this was where they had to leave the train. It was a bright morning with a feeling of spring in the air, coupled with the optimism which was prevalent now that the war was over. I left the train at Tilbury Riverside Station and was on board the *Samnesse* by about 9.30am. Tilbury was a busy passenger terminal for large liners and, when I stood on deck after dinner that evening, looking at the shipping on the busy river, it was with a feeling of elation. It was great to be back.

Similar to my previous ships, *Samite* and *Samforth*, the *Samnesse* had been built at the Bethlehem-Fairfield Shipyard in Baltimore. She was launched as the *Simon B Elliott*, but, similar to many of the Liberty Ships supplied to Britain under the Lease-Lend Agreement, her name had been changed before she made her maiden voyage. She was one of the ships which supported the Normandy Landings in June, 1944 and had been running to the Continent ever since. Now that the war was over, this was a very favourable run to be on and the mood on the ship was happy indeed. New articles, "for a period of six months in the Coasting, Home and/or Foreign Trade.....", were opened the day before I joined. The master was Captain Pearce and I signed on as 2nd R/O. The only snag was that I had to share my double-berth cabin on the bridge deck with a tall uncommunicative ex-[1]*Worcester*, 4th Mate who had already claimed the bottom bunk. I was told, however, that he needed only a further eight weeks of sea-time to allow him to sit for his 2nd Mate's ticket and after that I'd have the cabin to myself.

Apart from the larger passenger vessels, ships were now required to keep only an 8-hour human watch so that only one R/O was necessary. Holts, however, preferred to carry two R/Os and to have the No.1 as Purser. And 22-year-old Laurie Morgan, a pleasant chap from Harrogate, who was leaving the sea to join his fiancée in Buenos Aires, was No.1. Laurie, like me, was keen on music and had a piano accordion and a mouth organ. There was lots of music on the ship: Mr Farrow, the 3rd Engineer, had a radiogram and Bill Clow, the 3rd Mate from Kilmarnock who became a pal of mine, had a portable gramophone and lots of records.

One of the reasons why the *Samnesse* was such a happy ship was that everyone was in on the black market and I was soon acquainted of this fact. The ship had been running back and forth to Hamburg and although rationing in Britain was the same as it had been during the war, we had access to two things coveted by the Germans: cigarettes, which to us were duty-free and only 1/6d (7½p) for a tin of 50, and coffee.

The coffee had to be bought ashore and, although we were not allowed to bring it in at the dock gate, we could, ironically, post it to ourselves for delivery on board without questions being asked. Laurie had informed me of the drill, but Captain Pearce confused the issue by asking me to buy 4lbs for him and I rather resented this as his 'requirements' and my own, added to what I thought to be an inordinate amount of coffee for which to ask a

---

[1] HMS *Worcester* was a cadet training ship based at Greenhithe on the Thames.

grocer. I went up to Grays, Essex and into a large grocer's shop where I obtained 4lbs of coffee (for myself) and 4lbs of cocoa for the Captain. I had a supply of string and brown paper with me and made up two parcels in the GPO and posted them to the ship. When I entered my cabin, a day or so later, there was the pleasant aroma of coffee and my parcel was on the settee. Captain Pearce made a faint-hearted complaint to me, but it was a 'fait accompli'. I felt awkward about it, but, in the circumstances, didn't see why I should be landed with the less valuable cocoa.

3   HAMBURG

We sailed for Hamburg on Friday 22 March, 1946 and, as we were an H8 (eight hours human watch) ship, the requirement was that a radio officer should be on watch from 0800 to 1000, 1200 to 1400, 1600 to 1800 and 2000 to 2200 hours GMT with the auto-alarm on at all other times. It was therefore totally unnecessary for a watch to be kept during the night, but Laurie had me on from 0200 to 0800 and from 1600 to 1800 gmt while he kept the 0800 to 1000, 1200 to 1400 and 2000 to 2200 watches and I just accepted this. Throughout my time at sea, I, sometimes, felt off-colour when I went out into a rough sea after a spell ashore. But, although the sea was not very rough on that crossing, I was, for the one and only time, physically sick and vomited into the waste bin during my first night on watch. When Laurie relieved me at 8am, he said that I looked green. I certainly felt it, but soon recovered.

We sailed up the Elbe and docked on the morning of Sunday 24 March and our first objective was to get our coffee ashore. Laurie and I had it hidden inside the transmitter, but as the wireless room absolutely stank with coffee, we laughingly said we'd leave two empty cups to explain the aroma. And when it was rumoured that the ship was going to be searched, we decided to get our contraband ashore as quickly as possible.

Laurie knew where to sell our coffee and we experienced no difficulty in leaving the deserted dock area. Carrying our parcels, we walked through dark streets in an area of tenements and located the tenement where a dock foreman lived. We mounted the stairs and were admitted into the foreman's house where his wife and other women were present. Laurie received payment for his coffee, but when I said that I would like a camera, I was told that, while I could have one, I could have a much better model if I brought the same amount of coffee next trip. I agreed to this and left without payment or any written agreement.

The RAF had made an awful mess of Hamburg and, when I say awful, it is using the true meaning of the word, as God knows what it must have been like to experience the fury of the air raids. 55,000 people had been killed and more than half the City destroyed so that it was impossible to walk down a single street without seeing gutted-out buildings and heaps of rubble. What had been dock sheds were mere pieces of charred wood and ships lay where they had been sunk at their moorings. Our two midshipmen and I boarded the ss *D.Dammon* which, I was told, had been on the New York run before the war. The ship had been stripped of everything she possessed, but I came across a very small rusted tin inside which was a folded, soiled, 24-hour travel pass issued in Stettin (now Szczecin), in Poland, to Messe-Steward Johann Schmidt. The ship had one lifeboat still intact. We tried to launch it, but having got it to within inches of the water, could get it no further. The dock, however, was tidal and when we returned the next day, we succeeded in our efforts. The boat was, of course, of no use to us, but when some British soldiers, messing about in the harbour in another boat, came along, we offered it to them and they were pleased to have it.

On my next trip ashore, I went into town on a truck with exuberant RN matelots who took great delight in pointing down at the front of every German vehicle which followed us. The gesture was meant to convey to the driver of the vehicle that he had a puncture and, when he stopped, a howl of derision went up from the 'juvenile' delinquents.

Single-deck trams ran fairly frequently and were free to all Allied personnel, but I usually walked into town, past the enormous statue of Otto von Bismarck, the architect of German unity. By this time, the German people had become accustomed to having British and Americans in their city and I formed the opinion that, while some were friendly and others apathetic, the majority had no great love of us. And this was hardly surprising considering the death and destruction which had been wrought upon them.

The majority of Hamburg's citizens were reasonably well dressed although their clothes seemed a bit old-fashioned. There was very little in the shops and food was in short supply with each person receiving a ration of, roughly, 1000 calories worth a day which was considered to be half the amount necessary to maintain health. Fuel was scarce and I saw people hauling home branches of trees for their fires. There was no street lighting, but this differed from the wartime 'blackout' in that lights were freely displayed from windows. And, complementary to the lack of street lighting, there was a curfew in force which required German civilians to be off the streets by 10.15pm. After that time the streets were deserted except for the odd British serviceman or German policeman.

The Black Market was rife. People would approach you in the street to enquire if you had anything to sell, and coffee, cocoa and cigarettes, which could be exchanged for cameras, binoculars and radios, were more valuable than money. The German firm Hohner produced the best mouth organs. I had always regretted leaving my beautiful doubled-sided one on the "Queen Elizabeth", in 1943, and I was able to get a smaller replacement. The shop assistants who served me were courteous and I was struck by the beauty of many of the girls.

Hamburg was under British control and while the Germans were generally having a pretty rough time of it, many British and Americans were living the good life. This is not to suggest that there was anything wrong with that as, had the Nazis won the war, the (jack) boot would have been on the other foot with much more of a vengeance.

The rooms of the Hotel Atlantic, in the centre of the City, were used mainly by officers in transit, but the Hotel was the centre of the high life for all officers and others deemed to be of equivalent status such as consulate staff and UNRAA (United Nations Relief and Rehabilitation) officials. I was taken to the Atlantic by shipmates and spent three most enjoyable evenings there, in pleasant company, when all the food and drink we consumed was paid for by the proceeds from a few tins of duty-free cigarettes.

I had thought that the Southern Hotel in Baltimore, where I had stayed in 1944, was palatial until I saw the Atlantic which was absolutely magnificent. It had two large ballrooms with tables round the dance floors, a large grillroom and a large lounge and every one of these four rooms had an orchestra. There was a smaller lounge, a billiard room, a hairdressing salon and the longest bar in Europe. The decoration was superb, with the most beautiful chandeliers, and when I went there for afternoon tea, the waiters, wearing white gloves, used tongs to lift the cakes from silver salvers.

On my first evening there, we met a US Army lieutenant, whom my shipmates knew, and he brought two girls to our table. Both girls worked for the American section of UNRAA, but one was a slightly built Latvian. The well built American girl and the Lieut. were of the same mould, without inhibitions, and, when they sang "Roll Me Over In The Clover..." together, I formed an opinion about their relationship.

Two more from the *Samnesse* joined us on the second evening, but on the third and last evening there was a total of ten at our table and this was the best evening of all. The two UNRAA girls had departed for somewhere else in Germany, but four girls, on the staff of the US consulate, had joined us as had Maurice Turner, our 1st Mate. Sitting at a long table, we had an excellent meal with wine and then champagne to finish it off. Dancing at the hotel ended, roughly, when the curfew came into force and the hotel closed at 11pm.

We sailed on Thursday 28 March and ran into such thick fog that we dropped anchor at 10pm and lay, with our searchlights on, until the following morning. It was 3 o'clock in the afternoon of Monday, 1 April before we tied up alongside in Antwerp. The Agent brought us some mail and also the news that our next port-of-call was to be Immingham, in Lincolnshire. The Articles were deposited with and returned from the British Consulate General the following day. 6/6d was charged for this service and, stamped on them, 'Rate of Exchange for the conversion of seamen's wages; francs 176.50 = £1'.

4   ANTWERP

Antwerp lies about 55 miles southeast of the North Sea, on the estuary formed by the Rivers Scheldt, Meuse and Rhine. And, as the Wester Scheldt is within the Dutch province of Zeeland, ships have to pass through Dutch territorial waters in order to reach the port. The French-speaking Walloons call the town Anvers, but to the Flemings, who are in the majority in this Dutch speaking part of Belgium and who speak the Brabantian-Antwerp dialect, it is Antwerpen.

Brussels was only half-an-hour away, by electric train from Central Station, and I went there by myself on the Wednesday. I was in Brussels by 1.30pm and, on asking a passing Tommy about the places to see, he told me of a tram tour of the City which started at 2 o'clock from a nearby location. I hastily joined this tour which was exclusive and free to Allied personnel and excellent apart from the fact that the tram was unable to stop for more than a few minutes at points of interest as otherwise it would have held up other trams on regular routes. I had borrowed Bill Clow's camera, but it was only from a distance that I was able to photograph the building behind which Nurse Edith Cavell had been shot by the Germans on 12 October, 1915 and who, according to the monument on her grave beside Norwich Cathedral, "gave her life for *England*", and not *Britain*. The tram went all round Brussels and for 7 or 8 miles outside the City and, when the tour was over, I tramped round some of central places again. I spent time in the Grand Place and at the Mannikin Fountain, watched the ladies sitting in shop doorways making the beautiful Brussels lace, and climbed to the top of the Column of Congress which commemorates Belgium's declaration of independence, from the Netherlands in 1830. At the foot of the Column is the Tomb of the Belgian Unknown Warrior, similar to the one in Paris, and where a gas torch burns continuously. I had acquired a Forces leaflet which incorporated a plan of the City, places of interest and entertainments and, under the section headed 'Do's and Dont's, all ranks were ordered to salute the Tomb.

Light was failing and I was now tired and hungry. From the booklet, I saw that the British Officers' Club was in Rue d'Arlon and was in its vicinity when I asked an RAF Pilot Officer for directions. He knew where it was, but said that the Allied Officers' Club was better and, as he too was bent on having a meal, we went there and had our meal together. The restaurant was large and palatial, but not busy, with many waiters standing around. I settled for the table d'hôte menu and enjoyed an excellent meal which cost little or nothing. My companion, however, went for à la carte dishes, which included oysters, and, when he was presented with a bill which staggered him, exclaimed, "I was hungry, but not that hungry!" He then tried to persuade me to go with him on a round of the nightclubs, but I declined, caught the 9.30 train back to Antwerp and was back on board by 10.45pm.

I planned on visiting Ghent on the Saturday, but, due to the ship shifting its berth, lunch was late and when I got to the Central Station at 2 o'clock, I learned that the next train wouldn't get me there until 5.30pm. This was useless so I decided to go the following day. But it turned out that I never did see Ghent as Midshipman Taffy Davies approached me later in the day to ask if I would accompany him in an attempt locate his brother's grave.

Taffy's brother was a soldier and only 19 when he was killed, just over the Belgian border, in the Netherlands, in September 1944 and the information given his parents was that he was buried in a British cemetery "7 miles north-west of Maesek (Maaseik) at a place called Hasselt". We studied the map. Hasselt was our target. We rose at 5.45am on Sunday 7 April and took the 7.10am train to Brussels where we had to change, first of all, for Louvain (Leuven).

As the train to Louvain didn't leave until 8.42am, we killed time by walking the deserted streets of Brussels before returning to have a coffee in the station buffet as we had had no breakfast. When we paid for the coffees, we expected to receive two cups of coffee as we would have done in Britain, but a percolator was brought to our table and the coffee dripped so slowly that we became anxious and thought that we would have to forego the beverage in order to catch our train.

We arrived in Louvain about 9.20am and had an hour to spare before the train left for Hasselt at 10.22am. We had a wander round Louvain, which had been badly damaged by shellfire, and I took several snapshots. We caught the train to Hasselt and arrived there about 12.15pm.

Although it was Sunday, Hasselt's streets were lined with people who had turned out to witness a cycle race. We had planned on seeing the British Town Major, but, when we enquired of a spectator, we learned that there were no British in the town. Our first priority, however, was to get some food. It looked as if every place were closed, but when Taffy asked two Belgian Army lieutenants where we could get a meal and in the course of conversation explained why we were there, they said there was no British cemetery in Hasselt, but to come and have lunch in their mess.

When Taffy's folks had first received word of their son's death, the letter had said 'near Bree' and then, later, 'at Hasselt'. The officers, who had immediately involved themselves in our quest, produced a road map, said that they would requisition a staff car, which turned out to be a large spacious vehicle with a driver, and go with us to try Bree.

When we got to Bree, about 30 miles from Hasselt, we learned that there were a few houses in the vicinity which also went under the name of Hasselt and weren't long in arriving there. It was a lovely afternoon. We heard singing coming from the church and people standing near the church informed us that the bodies of 80 British soldiers had recently been removed from a nearby cemetery and taken to one in Burgleopold (Leopoldsburg). Before continuing our journey, we stood in the middle of the deserted road in the hamlet and had our picture taken with a family, which included several children, who came out of their house to assist us.

After enquiries, at Burgleopold, we eventually came to a small cemetery in a wood and found the grave. I took several pictures before wandering off to leave Taffy alone with his brother.

We were taken back to the officers' mess, in Hasselt (major), for tea and where our benefactors, Lieutenants Gerres and Willems, introduced us to all the other officers who made us feel welcome. They then escorted us to the railway station and saw us on the train. It had been a most memorable day, during which people had stared at our unfamiliar uniforms and, during the round trip from Hasselt back to Hasselt, we had covered a distance of about 75 miles. When we took our leave from the lieutenants, they shook our hands and said "Goodbye, sir". We expressed our thanks, but knew it was impossible to thank them. It is rarely that one experiences such kindness and, most certainly, without their assistance we would never have found the grave. I later enclosed an inadequate gift of cigarettes with a letter of thanks.

Tugs came to assist us from our berth at 4am on Tuesday 9 April, 1946 and we docked, in Immingham, around noon the following day.

5   IMMINGHAM AND LONDON

As I had paid off the *Samforth*, in Immingham, six months previously, this was my second visit to the port and, on arrival, received a letter from the Passenger Department of the LMS Co. in Dundee offering me £50 in settlement of my claim for my stolen luggage. I spent the afternoon replying to this letter and rejected their paltry offer. The terminus of the LNER (London & North Eastern Railway) Grimsby & Immingham Electric Railway was conveniently located at the dock gate and the return fare to Grimsby was 1/6d (7½p). In the evening, Bill Clow and I travelled to Grimsby and went to the pictures.

Since my unpleasant experience with the Customs searcher at the conclusion of the voyage of the *Samite* in October, 1944, who had abused me for having a few ounces of pipe tobacco over the limit although we had been away for 16 months and had been bombed and torpedoed, I had an understandable antipathy towards the breed. But the searcher who came on board in Immingham was a pleasant chap and I was seated on the settee in Lauries's cabin when Laurie welcomed him in with the offer of a drink.

At 22, Laurie was already an astute businessman, the acknowledged master smuggler of the *Samnesse*, and it was an education to watch him at work. A sailor had bought a piano accordion in Hamburg and, for a commission, had asked Laurie to get it ashore for him. Laurie had his own accordion in his wardrobe, but the sailor's accordion was under his small desk and he sat with his feet on it. The searcher did not search the cabin and, after the preliminary greetings, Laurie produced a pink customs slip, dated some months previously, to allow an accordion, on which duty had been paid, to taken ashore in London. The searcher then told Laurie that the slip was valid only at the time of issue. This information came 'as a complete surprise' to Laurie. A new pink customs slip was issued, allowing the accordion to be taken ashore without 'further' payment of duty.

I doubt very much if the searcher were 'taken in' as I never again met a Customs official like the searcher who humiliated me at the end of the *Samite's* voyage. Customs officers did their best for us and, looking at the Custom's manifest on which we declared dutiable articles, they would put words into our mouths and ask "Where did you buy it? Aden? (Singapore? Hong Kong?)" as articles purchased in a British colony were subject to a lower rate of duty. But my first experience of the Customs frightened me so that, throughout my time at sea, I never attempted to smuggle anything as this was a mugs' game when dealing with such reasonable officials.

I hoped to get home for a short leave, from London, but as this was doubtful, I posted home the rug I had bought in Antwerp. I also posted home my dhobi (washing), for which I apologised and asked my mother to sent it to a laundry which, of course, she did not do, nor did I expect her to! We expected to be in Tilbury for a week or so and I hoped that this was sufficient time for her to return my clothes to me and I asked her to send them c/o [2]BROMT, Shed 20, Tilbury Docks.

We left Immingham on Friday 12 April and arrived in Tilbury at noon the following day. And, as it seemed that I could depart for a few days at home, I was dressed ready to go. Laurie had applied to the Argentinean Consulate for a visa, some 6 months previously, and visited the Consulate to hasten his application. Our hopes, however, were dashed when the ship was not taken into the docks, but given a berth in the tidal river with its 22 feet rise and fall. This meant that half the crew had always to be on board and that the deck and engineering departments were kept on normal sea-watches. There was no work done by the dockers over the weekend and the discharging of our cargo of army vehicles did not begin until Monday morning.

I travelled into London on the Monday and in the evening went to see the operetta 'Song Of Norway', based on the life and music of Edvard Grieg, at the Palace Theatre in Shaftesbury Avenue. The show ended at about 9.15pm, but it was 12.15am before I was back on board the ship. The 3-hour journey incorporated a change of trains at Barking, where I had an hour's wait, and a 20-minute walk from Tilbury Riverside Station, through the docks, to the ship.

On Saturday morning, my dhobi arrived back from Dundee together with a letter saying that the rug had arrived safely.

On our arrival at Tilbury, we were told that, after two years of running to the Continent, the *Samnesse* was being taken off the run: rumour was that she was to make at least one voyage to the Far East to replace a ship being laid up for repairs. The whole crew were to pay-off the following week, but some would be rejoining for the subsequent voyage and I expected to be one of them. Laurie was one who was not rejoining and I regretted this as we got on so well together. Within a few days, however, the rumour regarding the ship's run was scotched and we were told that the ship was

---

[2] The letters stood for something concerning motor transport.

going to the Mediterranean and perhaps to Greece. I was pleased about this and speculated that I might, at long last, meet up with my pal, David Cathro, who was now an RAF Warrant Officer stationed in Athens and whom I had narrowly missed in several places during the war. I also speculated that, as the 4th Mate was not rejoining, I would have the cabin to myself and that, in July, my pay would be increased to £21-10/- a month. Maurice Turner paid-off on 20 April and a 'relief' Mate joined. I paid-off on Wednesday 24 April. I was told that I was to rejoin the ship, but that I was free to go home on leave. Taking only my grip, containing the bare necessities, I travelled to Dundee on the 9.45pm, overnight, train from Kings Cross when my companion in the sparse sleeping compartment, where we were provided with only a bench and a blanket, was a customs officer! As there was no bathroom in our house, I had a bath at the Dundee Municipal Baths, beside the shore, before going home.

And so ended a most enjoyable short trip on the *Samnesse*, during which I had gone to a great deal of trouble, and expense, to smuggle a present of coffee to an unknown family in Hamburg.

Postscript: My few days at home allowed me to celebrate my 21st birthday with family and friends and, on the evening of the day following my return home, I received the following telegram (Reply Paid to the tune of 1/-) from Holts. 'REJOIN SAMNESSE LONDON NOT LATER THAN TWO PM TUESDAY THIRTIETH TELEPHONE ALBERT DOCK 2977 ARRIVAL LONDON ACKNOWLEDGE = ODYSSEY'.

Another adventure was about to begin!

6   PROMOTION

When I returned to the ship on Tuesday, 30 April, 1946, I found Laurie still on board and it was he who broke the news to me that I was to sail as No.1. I could hardly believe it; it was only a matter of months since Holts had dismissed me as a redundant 3rd Sparks. But with the elation came the realisation that I had little idea as to my duties as Purser. Laurie also informed me that a new Master had joined and that he wanted me to move in with the 2nd Sparks, in the double berth cabin next door, so that a passenger could have a cabin to himself to Piraeus. And it was Laurie who put into my mind that I could resist this by saying that this was contrary to Board of Trade regulations as the Auto Alarm Bell was in the 1st R/O's cabin.

Captain Ffoulkes was angry when I explained why I could not vacate my cabin. "Good heavens man", he said, "you can hear the bell all over the ship". But, as I remained adamant, he resorted to blackmail and said that, as he had been instructed to give the passenger a cabin in the officers' accommodation, the only other solution was to give him the 2nd R/O's cabin and to accommodate the 2nd R/O on the crew's deck.

When Tony Raven, the 2nd R/O, came on board, I informed him of the situation. He went immediately to see Captain Ffoulkes and the problem was solved by Tony suggesting that the passenger share his cabin. Subsequently, Captain Ffoulkes did not hold a grudge against me and was one of the finest men I ever met.

On the previous short voyage, many of our crew came from the Greater London area, but now the majority were from Merseyside. The Articles had been opened in Birkenhead on 26 April, but, together with others, I signed on in Tilbury on 1 May.

My first problem, as Purser, was not long in appearing. 49-year-old C Griffin, AB, had not turned up to sign on with the rest of us and I had the job of signing him on the following day. Entering his particulars in the Articles and witnessing his signature was easy enough, but the problem came when he asked for an advance of £6 in favour of the lady with whom he lived. I had never heard of [3]Advance Notes and did not even know if I

---

[3] Although Advance Notes were commonplace, they were entirely at the discretion of the Master and could not legally be demanded by seamen.

were empowered to grant the request so that I expressed my reluctance to do so. Mr Griffin then became so agitated that, after finding out how to go about it, I issued the Note. My judgment, based solely on his anxiety, proved to be correct.

The very next day, I was called upon to see to the discharge of James Collins, a 42-year-old fireman from Liverpool. Mr Collins was taken so ill that a doctor was called to examine him. The doctor diagnosed malaria. Mr Collins was landed into Tilbury Seamen's Hospital and we were left short of a fireman.

Although I had sailed with 1st RO/Pursers for nearly three years, I had received no training whatsoever in the Purser's job and had little idea of what a purser did other than look after the wage accounts of the crew. I was desperate for information and when a clerk from the London office came on board, I endeavoured to extract as much information as I could from him. He could not, of course, offer much assistance, but, when I saw that he was carrying a book called Brown's Ships' Accounts and Concise Guide to Ships' Business, I eventually persuaded him to sell it to me. The book became my vade mecum and proved a godsend when I had nothing else to which to refer.

While the No.1 was responsible for the radio department, he did not keep a watch and was almost solely occupied with purser's duties. This situation, unique to Holts, stemmed from an economy measure brought in by Major the Hon. Leonard Cripps, a manager of the Company and the elder brother of Sir Stafford, during the Depression of the 1930s when all companies were experiencing difficulty. At that time, only one R/O was carried and, as it was deemed that he had little to do, but listen, Cripps added the purser's work to his duties. R/Os were in no position to object as, had they done so, they would have been replaced and joined the dole queue. It was a time when everyone in a job was extremely fortunate and men with masters' tickets were reduced to sailing as deckhands. By the end of the Second World War, however, the situation had radically changed. Officers, in all departments, were scarce and it was impossible for one man to do both jobs anyway. Another economy measure brought in by Cripps was that only one egg was to be served at breakfast on all ships, instead of the traditional two. This followed the suggestion of a master, henceforth known as 'One-Egg Turner', who claimed that, with a crew of fifty and eggs a halfpenny each, £60 was saved in the year on one vessel and about £3000 for the fleet.

7   SHIPMATES

Captain A.J. Ffoulkes was 52 and a small stocky, clean-shaven man. He had gone to sea, as an apprentice in sail, in 1909, and had his Extra Master's (Square Rig) Certificate when he was only about 26. He had made many voyages round the Horn to the west coast of South America, (I remember him speaking of the sailing ship *James Kerr*) but, as the age of sail was over, had transferred into steamships and had become a junior officer with Blue Funnel. I did not know all this at the time, but learned about his early life when, with my family, I spent holidays in his home, at 3 Speedwell Road, Birkenhead, during the hot summers of 1975/76 when he was in his mid-eighties. At the time, I knew only that he had held a shore post during the war and had lost a son. I assumed that his son had been in the Forces, but learned later that 'Laddie' had been killed by a car when cycling in Birkenhead during the 'blackout'. Although born in Liverpool, Captain Ffoulkes had been raised in North Devon so that he regarded himself as a Devon man and had a fine Devon accent. Again, at the time, I did not know that the *Samnesse* was his first command, but could see that he was returning to sea like 'a dog with two tails'. I think he came to looked upon me like a son and we sometimes went ashore together.

M.G. (Machine Gun) Turner, aged 40, had his Master's Certificate and was a slim pleasant man with a very furrowed brow. Divorced from his first wife, he had recently married a young lady twenty years his junior whom I met when she visited the ship prior to sailing. Mr Turner was obviously happy with the new arrangement and from time to time impressed upon me his view that the woman I should marry was just being born! Although it would not have been long before he was given a command, MG's ambition was to settle down in a shore job so that he could be with his wife. He always called me Mac, but, in deference to his age rather than to his seniority, I addressed him as Mr Turner.

E.A. Pennington, the 2nd Mate, was a rather shy and unassuming man aged 28 who had only his 2nd Mate's Ticket when the majority of Holt's 2nd Mates had their Mate's. Ernest had been a Lieutenant [4]RNR during the war and this was his first trip back with Holts. He became my best friend on the ship so that we often went ashore together and, like Mr Turner, he always called me Mac. He was married and had a small daughter. His

---

[4] At that time, RNR personnel were merchant seamen, but the term now includes those who would have previously been RNVR.

home was in Portsmouth and his father was a retired Master. But, also like Mr Turner, his heart was no longer 'in the sea' and wanted to 'escape' into a shore job. He was interested in architecture and, when we were ashore together, we would climb over building sites where he examined bricks and other aspects of the structure. The majority of the officers I sailed with became disillusioned with life at sea, but it was perhaps more difficult for deck officers to find employment ashore. Some were fortunate enough to get jobs as pilots and harbour masters, but the majority had to retrain in order to enter other professions. Ernest blotted his copybook with Captain Ffoulkes by objecting to turnout to do a job after he had completed his watch. This was anathema to Ffoulkes with his hard sailing-ship training and, of course, every man, and particularly every officer, could be called upon to turnout at any time.

George Brydges, age 21, was our uncertificated 3rd Mate and a 'son of the manse' from Farnham, Surrey.

Our two midshipmen, Alan Curry and Peter Pratt, were both 19. The latter had a penchant for the ladies and I never had much to do with him, but Alan, the senior, used to frequently visit me in my cabin during the evenings and I came to know something of his background. During the war, he had gone to the RN training college in Dartmouth and then to sea as a midshipman, RN. On his uniform jacket he wore the Oak Leaves testifying to his bravery when he had been 'mentioned in dispatches'. Alan's father was an admiral, serving in Hong Kong, his brother was an engineer commander on King George V and his girlfriend had the title of Honourable. As, throughout the voyage, Alan borrowed my electric iron, which I had adapted to the ship's 120 volt DC supply, I eventually said to him, "If your father's an admiral, your brother's a commander, RN and your girl's an Honourable, why can't you afford your own electric iron"?"! Alan was a tall slim fair-haired lad with no great sense of humour. He never seemed to be particularly happy and I have no idea why he came to be in the Merchant Service.

J. Quayle, the Chief Engineer, aged 49, had a 1st Class Certificate in Steam and was a large, balding, strong-looking and forceful man who wore glasses.
The 2nd Engineer was R. McNeill. He was 30 and had his 1st Class in both Steam and Motor and was a quiet pleasant efficient-looking man. I remember him for the very silly reason that he was embarrassed at wearing a jockstrap when he entered the showers with me one day and asked if I had ever worn one! Only the Chief and 2nd Engineers were certificated.

J. Steadman, the 3rd Engineer was 31 years old. Bill Harrison, age 23, was the 4th. He was a small cheerful lad from the Wigan area and became a good friend. J.M. Walker, age 21, signed on as Assistant Engineer.

Tony Raven, the 2nd R/O, was a few months older than I was and the product of a broken home. His father had been in the RAF and, when the parents broke up, Tony was separated from his two sisters and brought up in a school for orphans. When he was 14, he left the school to undergo a year's pre-sea training on a training ship which, I believe, was owned by the Bibby Line, after which he went to sea as a deck boy on a Bibby Liner. Tony told me that he was on the bridge of the ship when someone had asked a question and, when he had been foolish enough to answer, the Captain had struck him a blow which carried him across the deck. He had already been torpedoed when, in 1942, he managed to get time off and, using money he had saved, attended Liverpool Wireless College to study for a Special Ticket. In February, 1943, he returned to sea, as a radio officer, and his previous voyage had been to Curacao on the Shell tanker *Cistula*. Previous to that, he had served on a Lamport and Holt ship and I still have the sketches which he gave me and which he had drawn on Lamport and Holt menu cards. He would like to have studied art, but, when he had submitted samples of his work to the Principal of the Liverpool School of Art, he was advised to keep art as a hobby. Tony sometimes recited the lines "quote the raven, nevermore" from Edgar Allan Poe's poem 'The Raven'. And, in later years, I remembered his philosophical statement that you sometimes have to go back a step in order to make progress in life when I had to do just that. Tony sometimes spoke of a gentleman, who had some connection either with the orphan school he had attended or the training ship, and who had given him help and guidance. This man owned the small Manx Marine Radio Co., and I later met him in his office in the Liver Building. It was not surprising that, due to his experience, which eclipsed my own, Tony started off by trying to tell me what to do, but this difficulty was soon overcome and I never sailed with a better shipmate. I was surprised and irritated, however, to find that, because he had more sea-time than I had, he signed on at £21-10/- a month while my wage was £18, plus a bonus of £1 a month for being purser. I took this up with Ffoulkes who said that he had noticed this, but further irritated me by suggesting that perhaps a mistake had been made and that Tony should have been the No.1! Tony's 2nd Class Certificate was dated two days after mine, and Holts had no doubt given him the junior post because it was his first trip with them. A particular attribute of Tony's was that he made a point of addressing all ratings as Mr which he said was how they would be addressed in any other civilian occupation.

F. W. Sawle, the Chief Steward, was a somewhat rotund man of 39 and Mr Godwin, the 2nd Steward and Captain's 'Tiger', was six years his senior. The term Captain's 'Tiger' was the unofficial title given to the steward who attended the [5]'Old Man' and, on every ship I sailed, this was the 2nd Steward. Although Godwin didn't wear glasses, he had a bad squint in one eye which gave him rather an odd appearance and, as he had to pass my door to reach Ffoulkes' quarters, he frequently stopped for a chat.

Some of the crew were regular Blue Funnel men, but many had been taken from the Pool and had served with other companies. H. Bevins, our 54-year-old Bosun, was regular Blue Funnel and was of the solid, reliable type, which I always sailed with. The Deck Boy, always referred to as the Bosun's 'Peggy', was Frederick Clive Crampthorn, age 16, who had made his first trip to sea on our short trip to the Continent. Paid at the rate of only £5 a month, he was the lowest paid on the ship and the Bosun was seldom seen without his 'Peggy' in attendance. Prior to joining the *Samnesse*, Captain Ffoulkes had spent a period in charge of the Outward Bound Sea School at Aberdovey. Fred Crampthorn, a tall, lanky, shy lad had attended the School so that Ffoulkes knew him and, meaning to be kind, frequently embarrassed him by referring to his time at Aberdovey when Fred would stand silently and blush.

We carried 2 ABs (Able Bodied Seamen), 3 EDHs (Efficient Deck Hands), 2 SOSs (Senior Ordinary Seamen) and 2 JOSs (Junior Ordinary Seamen). The Bosun was paid £16 a month, the ABs and EDHs £14, the SOSs £10 and the JOSs £8-10/-. The Carpenter, H. Gastall, age 36, was paid £17-5/- a month.

The Donkeyman, the Bosun's equivalent in the engine-room, was T. Grealey, age 32; paid £15.12.6d a month. We carried 4 Greasers and 5 Firemen. The Greasers were paid £15 a month and the Firemen £14-10/-.

The Chief Cook was F. Parry and the 2nd Cook and Baker was E. Knight. They were paid £18.10/- and £15 a month respectively. The Carpenter, Bosun, Donkeyman and Chief Cook were all Petty Officers. The Chief Steward was also a Petty Officer, but wore officers' uniform with 2 sharply wavy gold bands. Chief Stewards always lived in the officers'

---

[5] The term had nothing to do with age; every master was referred to, behind his back, as the 'Old Man'. The same term was also used by operators on ship and coastal radio stations, but in this case it was a method of showing friendship to those with whom we communicated.

accommodation, but never ate in the saloon or mixed with the officers. Their situation was somewhat unique and I believe that they were housed in the officers' accommodation to keep them apart from the crew who could, sometimes, be antagonistic towards them. Some years after I had left the sea, they became Catering Officers.

Crew overtime rates were: Bosun and Donkeyman – 2/3d (11¼p) per hour. 2nd and Assistant Stewards, ABs, and EDHs – 2/- (10p). SOSs, JOSs and boys –1/- (5p). Their leave pay entitlement was 2 days, at their basic rate, for every month on Articles. A minimum of 15 days earned 1 day's leave as did 29 days.

Other monthly rates of pay were: 1st Mate - £34.5/-. 2nd Mate - £29. 3rd Mate - £20.5/-.
Chief Engineer - £48. 2nd Engineer - £34.5/-. 3rd Engineer - £27.10/-. 4th Engineer - £24. Assistant Engineer (1st Voyage) - £19. Chief Steward - £21.15/-. Second Steward - £16.10/-.

The War Risk Payment, subject to income tax, was still paid in addition to salaries - £10 a month for those over 18 and £5 if under that age.

Now that the war was over, there were no longer DEMS gunners on board and all armament had been removed from the ship. Our total complement was 39 of which the majority were young.

8   THE PASSAGE TO PIRAEUS

We sailed on Saturday 4 May, 1946 and, when we momentarily stopped at a lock, B. Jenkins, a young chubby and cheerful fireman, climbed up a rope ladder to replace Mr Collins. I had heard of 'pier-head jumps', but none can surpass that of Mr Jenkins as, minutes later, we were 'at sea'. The next day was my brother's 17th birthday and the telegram, sent via Northforelandradio (call sign GNF), and with economy in mind, read only "HAPPY BIRTHDAY ERIC = IAN". In the evening, when we were well down the Channel, I was polishing my shoes in my cabin when Captain Ffoulkes came in and laughing commented on the fact that he had never seen anyone cleaning their shoes on the first day at sea.

Although I was obliged to take over in the wireless room only when it was necessary to relieve Tony for a meal, I elected to keep the first daily watch as I thought this fair when we were running for the Ministry of Transport and cargo work was not included in the purser's duties. Both had all night in bed and this was a luxury which neither of us had previously enjoyed.

We were asleep when the auto-alarm bell in my cabin startled us into wakefulness during our second night at sea. In pyjamas and bare feet, we raced to the wireless room, switched on the receiver, and waited for an SOS message to be sent by a ship in distress. We waited for some time, but heard no message so that we reset the auto-alarm and returned to our beds. We had just time to fall asleep, when the bell went again and, again, we raced to switch on the receiver. But there was still no SOS so that the device was reset and we went back to bed. We were in the vicinity of Lands End and, when the bell went off for a third time, I called up Landsendradio (call sign GLD) and asked if there was a ship in distress. The operator said that he had not heard anything so that we deduced that our auto-alarm was being activated by static. Most unprofessionally, we switched off the auto-alarm and passed the remainder of the night undisturbed.

Our sole passenger, who occupied the top bunk in Tony's cabin, was Mr Morphy of the firm which made irons and other electrical equipment. At my first sight of him, I put him down as an Army officer and he had been a major, serving in East Africa during the war. He was a pleasant man, but his sleeping habits did not endear him to Tony. He snored loudly, but this was a minor inconvenience against the hours which he kept. He had a theory about 'sleep' and claimed that, if a graph were drawn, it would show that only the first hours would appear steeply and the later, unnecessary, hours horizontal. This was why, he said, he preferred not to sleep too long during the night and to have another rest in the afternoon. He would get up at 4 or 5am, waken Tony and offer him a cheese sandwich. He would then return to bed about 6.30am and fall immediately to sleep while Tony was left staring up at the bunk on which Morphy snored. Major Morphy was an interesting man. He spent many hours in my cabin and I enjoyed his company. He spoke Greek, German and Italian and his wife and children were to join him in Greece, where he had been born and had lived before the war and his brother was the Blue Funnel agent in Piraeus. Tony was of the opinion that, while a learned man, Major Morphy probably would not know how to darn a sock. And this was substantiated when we saw him struggling to iron a shirt.

We enjoyed good weather through the Bay of Biscay and it was equally good as we sailed in the Mediterranean. Captain Ffoulkes' had a son who was a Petty Officer in the Royal Navy and Ffoulkes knew that he was on a ship heading for home and likely to pass us in the Med. He asked me to keep a lookout for her 'on the air' and when we did locate her, father and son exchanged greetings.

It was still early days after the war and I doubt if anyone possessed a personal wireless set. There was, however, a general coverage receiver, which may have been an RCA AR-88, in the wireless room. I led a lead from it into my cabin, connected a pair of earphones to the end of the lead and placed an earphone in a tumbler to give resonance. When people came into my room they would ask where the music was coming from! In the Mediterranean, we listened as usual to the Overseas Service of the BBC, but also to the AFN (American Forces Network) station located somewhere in Europe. I liked the AFN which broadcast information, plays, music and news to the US Forces. The announcer would give his name as Pfc or Cpl So and So and state that the news came from the wires of the AP, UP and INS (Associated Press, United Press and International News Service). The tune which I associate with that time is 'The Girl That I Marry' from Irving Berlin's 'Annie Get Your Gun' which was currently being performed on the stage in New York.

Although the job of purser was an onerous one when the main part of the job was involvement in cargo work, it was not at all onerous on the *Samnesse* although, as a new boy, I did not appreciate how fortunate I was. But, without training or experience, I spent many hours studying Brown's Ships' Accounts and trying to get to grips with the job which consisted of the following.

From the Articles, which showed each man's rate of pay, I made out a wages book with an account for each man, apart from the Master. Only a few had been issued with Advance Notes, but almost everyone had signed an Allotment Note stipulating that a certain sum was to be paid monthly, half-monthly or weekly, by Holt's to the person nominated. Other deductions were income tax, insurance, contributions to the National Union of Seamen, Holt's pension fund or the Merchant Navy Officers' Pension Fund and the Bosun contributed to the Merseyside Hospital (1d in the £1) Scheme. The MNOPF had been in existence only since 1937, but in 1946 there was no similar pension scheme for ratings.

As the Articles of the *Samnesse* were opened on 26 April, 1946, prior to the passing of the National Insurance Act later in the year, we were still under the previous insurance regulations which stipulated that only those below a certain salary were required to make payments. The result of this was that only the ratings paid insurance contributions.

When all deductions had been made, I worked out the daily net rate and multiplied this by the number of days as the voyage progressed so that I knew what each man could draw, after taking his Steward's Account into consideration. Cash was never used for purchases, such as drink and tobacco, made against the latter account and payment was made by signing pink chits.

A day or two before arriving in port, I, or Tony, took a sheet round on which each man indicated how much he wanted to 'draw' on arrival. When we arrived in port, I gave the Agent a note showing the global sum which I required and which he provided in reasonably small units in order to assist distribution. The money was, of course, paid in local currency and while I had a rough idea of the rate of exchange, either before or as soon as we entered port, it was only when we had left that Captain Ffoulkes informed me as to the exact rate. He knew this because it was required by law that his copy of the Articles, and the apprentices' indentures, had to be lodged with the British Consulate in a foreign port or with Customs authorities in a colonial port. And, when the Articles were returned to him, the rate of exchange was stamped on them. I may say that the cash which each man left available to himself was not at all linked to his rate of pay as most senior officers left allotments which left them extremely short of spending money.

Another part of the job was meeting port officials and providing crew lists. These lists, showing the name, age and rank/rating of all on board, were always required. One crew list was never enough so that I made as many carbon copies as my typewriter could accommodate and kept a supply in hand. As we did not carry a surgeon, it was left to me to meet the Port Medical Officer who had to grant pratique before any physical contact was permitted with the shore. He made no medical examination, but merely asked me to sign a form guaranteeing that there was no infectious disease on board.

I was the ship's postmaster. We were tramping, so that our next port of call was never known until the last minute. This meant that our correspondents addressed their letters to Holts' office in Liverpool who forwarded them, en bloc, to the office of their agent in the port for which we were bound. The agent then gave the mail to me for distribution throughout the ship. Everyone brought their letters to me for posting and I passed them on to the agent. And, before we sailed from the port, he presented me with a list showing how much to debit each man's account.

I was also the ship's librarian, with Tony as my assistant. The Seafarers' Education Service had provided our library which consisted of about 300 books and, twice a week, when at sea, we made it available to all on board with allowances made for those on watch. And as seamen are avid readers, the SES allowed the exchange of libraries between ships in foreign ports.

Only a few months previously, I had been a 3rd Sparks expected to know little or nothing. Now 1st RO/Purser, I was expected to know everything.

The day before we were due to arrive in Piraeus, I asked Captain Ffoulkes if, when the time came, it were acceptable to transfer into khaki instead of whites. I think it was because he had not been at sea during the war that he was taken aback by the question and said it was a Company rule that whites should be worn. I explained that, because my luggage had been stolen from the luggage van of a train the previously November, I had hardly any whites and it turned out that many of the officers had mostly khaki. Fortunately, Mr Turner backed me up so that Ffoulkes compromised and said that he would prefer to see us in whites for the evening meal and wearing black ties! To some extent, Ffoulkes was living in the past. I kept the Official Log and when a crewmember committed a misdemeanour, Ffoulkes told me to log the incident and to record a [6]penalty which involved the loss of several days pay. Even with my

---

[6] The penalties which a master could impose were circumscribed and set down in the Articles. For a first offence, of any kind, the fine was 10/- (50p) and £1 for a

meagre knowledge of the regulations, I knew that he was not empowered to do this and, when I informed him, he stamped off in a rage.

We rounded Cape Maléa and docked in Piraeus at 8am on Tuesday, 14 May. The Agent brought a few letters on board, but I didn't receive any.

---

second or subsequent offence. If, on return to the United Kingdom, the Log showed that a master had exceeded the statutory penalty, the superintendent at the shipping office cancelled the penalty and the seaman got off scot-free.

9   PIRAEUS/ATHENS AND A REUNION

David Cathro, who had become a pal of mine when we worked together in Henry's office, was a Warrant Officer (First Class) Observer/Wireless Op. with 55 Squadron of the RAF somewhere near Athens. I had written him saying that we were heading for Piraeus and, on the afternoon of the day we docked, I set out to find him. Some RAF chaps were boarding a truck as I left the ship and they informed me that the squadron was located at Hassani Aerodrome, on the coast and about nine miles on the far side of Athens. I travelled to Athens on the electric train. The journey took only about 25 minutes and, after asking various people, I enquired at the RAF office in the City. RAF men were piling on to a bus/truck, at the door of the office, and when I learned that it was going to the 'drome, I climbed up among them.

When the truck arrived at the gate of the airport, it was stopped by the Greek guards on duty. But my companions on the truck merely hollered at the guards so that they stood aside and we drove in. It transpired that we were in the civilian airport and when I entered the office and asked the girl at the desk about 55 Squadron, she told me that the RAF station was at the far side of the 'drome. She said that I could not walk across the 'drome, but had to leave by the way I had entered and go along the coast road. Following her instructions, I walked along the coast road. It was a lovely day with the sea on my right and I was wondering if I were going in the right direction, when I came across some chaps in RAF uniform. They turned out to be Greeks, but the officer took me into their orderly room/hut and 'phoned 55 Squadron for me. I spoke to a chap who said that David had been expecting to hear from me, but that he had gone swimming and wouldn't be back until 5 o'clock. As it was only 3.15, I said that I did not want to hang around that long and to tell David to come down to the ship in the evening. I then walked back to the main part of the 'drome and caught the next RAF truck/bus into Athens.

It took me just about 20 minutes to climb the Acropolis which dominates the City and on which stands the Parthenon. On the way, I passed the Royal Palace (now the presidential residence) with its Greek guards in 'kilts', the University and the Steles of Olympian Zeus. I regretted not having a camera, but there was a photographer on the Acropolis and I had my photograph taken, sitting on a broken column, in front of the Parthenon. The photograph, produced on a postcard in about five minutes, cost me what would appear to be the enormous sum of 4000 drachma, but which was only 4/- (20p) as the [7]rate of exchange was 20,000 drachma to the £1. I persuaded the photographer to sell me the negative and he let me have it for the equivalent of 1/- (5p), but as it is also on a postcard and not like the usual negative, I have never known how to make use of it. It was about thirty years later that my father had his picture taken in the same spot and, perhaps, by the same photographer.

The shops of Athens were fairly well stocked with everything except clothes, but inflation was rampant and everything very expensive. To pay even an insignificant amount for anything, you had to peel off a number of dirty notes printed on poor thin paper.

I spent some time enjoying the wonderful atmosphere of the Acropolis and the views of the City, before descending the hill and having tea, consisting of egg, sausages and potatoes at the YMCA and which cost only 1/- (5p). I then walked to Omonia Square where I caught the electric train and arrived back in Piraeus about 7pm.

It was a 20-minute walk from the station to the ship and, as I walked through the docks, I half-expected to find David already on board. And he was - sitting in my cabin in the company of Tony and Bill Harrison. David and I had narrowly missed each other in Canada, Algeria and Egypt and it was great to meet up at last. Captain Ffoulkes, in shirt and braces, came and joined in the conversation and I must have neglected to introduce him as, when he left us, David asked who the 'old guy' was. And when I said that it was the Skipper, David said that he had suspected that he was. As he was not now flying and 'reduced' to being only a guard commander at the 'drome, David was 'browned off' (bored) with the RAF and looked forward to his demob (demobilisation/becoming a civilian again) which he

---

[7] As previously stated, it was the law that, when we called at a foreign port, the Agreement and Crew List, always referred to as the Articles, had to be deposited with the British Consulate. On the document, the Consulate recorded the date when it had been received by them, when it was returned to ship prior to sailing, any crew changes which had taken place in the port and the currency rate of exchange. A charge was made for this service and adhesive Consular stamps, carrying the King's head and showing the amount charged were affixed to the page. In Piraeus, the charge was 9/6d (47½p) and strangely enough, although George VI had been on the throne since 1938, it was the head of his father, George V, which was on all the stamps affixed to the Articles of the *Samnesse* throughout the voyage.

anticipated to be in July. I provided him with a light meal of sandwiches, a piece of my 21st birthday cake which I had saved for him and 200 cigarettes. I was badly in need of tropical kit and when he said that he could buy this for me at RAF stores, I asked him to get me three sets of khaki shorts, shirts and stockings. He left the ship about 10 o'clock as he had to catch the last 'bus' from Athens back to camp at 11.30pm and, as it was not safe to walk alone through the docks to Piraeus railway station after dark, Tony and I walked with him and saw him on the train. I arranged to meet him at the Warrant Officers' and Sergeants' Club in Athens at 2.30 the following afternoon and Tony and Bill were to join us in the evening. Although David had been stationed at Hassani for some time, he had not been to the Acropolis.

We met as planned and I found that I had stumbled into a significant day in Greek history. Germany invaded Greece in April, 1941 and Athens had been under Nazi rule until their forces withdrew from the City on 12 October, 1944. Since then Athens, and subsequently all Greece, had been under British military rule and now, on Wednesday, 15 May, 1946, the military were handing over to a civil government; elected only days previously and personified by the Archbishop Regent. The transfer was to take place in the Olympic Stadium and Athens was in turmoil with everyone wanting to be present at the ceremony. David, of course, was in uniform, but I had chosen to wear mufti so that, without him, the police, who were physically throwing people back, would not have allowed me to pass through the crowds. We climbed to the very top of the tiered steps of the [8]Stadium, from where we had a great view of the ceremony. British generals were present and we watched the symbolic hand-over to Archbishop Damaskinos. The atmosphere was 'electric' and, after the ceremony, performers kept the show going for hours and, after each 'turn', the crowd clapped in unison and not sporadically as we do in Britain. We left when we had seen enough, returned to the W/Os'/Sgts' Club for tea, and, afterwards, met Tony and Bill.

We went, first of all, to a nightclub. There was no entrance charge, but, as soon as we sat at a table, we were pestered to buy drinks. A hostess came to the table to 'encourage' us and we ordered drinks while, to keep us entertained, she sang 'J'attendrai' at David's request. We hastily left before

---

[8] The Stadium, which seats 70,000, is built entirely of pentelic marble. The original Stadium had been built in 330 BC, but a Greek millionaire, living in Alexandria, had had it rebuilt in time for the first of the modern Olympic Games in 1896.

the drinks arrived and ended the evening sitting under trees, in which lights were placed, at an open-air café halfway up a hill, eating eggs and chips. We descended the hill with me playing my mouth organ and the lads singing.

Some mail awaited our return to the ship and I received a letter from the Passenger Department of the LMS in Dundee increasing their offer, from £50 to £70, in compensation for my stolen luggage. I accepted the offer. But David was unable to provide the items of tropical khaki gear he had promised to get me from the RAF store as Wednesday had been declared a holiday.

Without any cargo, the *Samnesse* sailed for Genoa on Thursday, 16 May.

10   GENOA

We were to pass through the [9]Strait of Messina during the 4-8am watch on Saturday, 18 May. I wanted to see Mt Etna and, having asked Mr Turner to have me called at 4am, I stood with him on the bridge as we negotiated the Strait. The moon was still shining, but, within half-an-hour, it was broad daylight and Etna, although eighty miles away, could clearly be seen. Through Mr Turner's binoculars I could see snow on the summit and smoke rising from Europe's tallest active volcano. It was also a wonderful sight to see the Strait itself with Sicily to port and the Italian mainland to starboard. And the lights of Reggio, on the mainland, were still on as we passed. By 9am, smoking Stromboli, in the Lipari Islands, was on our starboard side and I marvelled that people could live on such a small island within the shadow of the active volcano. It was a fine passage in glorious weather and we docked, in Genoa, on Monday, 20 May.

Genoa stands on the narrow coastal plain between the mountains and the Gulf of Genoa and stretches into the foothills of the Ligurian Apennines. It is Italy's chief port, serving not only the country's industrial north, but also much of central Europe and is a fine city with a long maritime history.

I was surprised to find that the shops displayed more goods than those in Britain and limitless food could be had in restaurants. But prices were so high that the goods could not be bought by many of the people and, at every lunch time on the ship, women and children came on to the quay carrying baskets and begging for food. It was a distressing sight, but, every day, Ffoulkes had additional bread baked for them. Local elections had been held only weeks previously and a [10] referendum on the constitution was to be held on 2 June. Posters displaying the hammer and sickle or the clenched fist were to be seen all over the town and many buildings were defaced by electioneering graffiti. I was told that, at night,

---

[9] It was perhaps twenty years later that my father gave me a copy of an English translation of the Greek epic poem, the 'Odyssey', attributed to Homer, and from it learned that, by negotiating the Strait, we, like Odysseus, passed between the two monsters Scylla and Charybdis on not only this, but on three subsequent occasions. Scylla, now identified by a rock off the Italian mainland, lies almost directly opposite Charybdis; identified by a whirlpool, near the Sicilian shore.

[10] King Victor Emmanuel, who had been a mere puppet of Mussolini, had already abdicated in favour of his son. But as 54% of the population voted for a republic, it was the end of monarchy in Italy. And, in the general election, the Christian Democrats gained a clear majority of seats in the Constituent Assembly.

there were occasional street fights between Communist and Democrat supporters.

Prices were generally too high for us, but I bought a few small items as I wandered round admiring the many fine buildings. Of particular interest was the small house in which Christopher Columbus is reputed to have been born.

Tony and I entered a haberdasher's shop one afternoon and stood waiting our turn beside an extremely fat lady sitting on a chair by the door. Thinking that the lady would not understand what he said, Tony made a rude remark about her, but was embarrassed and ashamed when, a minute or so later, she addressed us in English. Sometimes we called at a shop in an arcade where we enjoyed a dish of whipped cream. The arcade was beautiful with a high glass roof to allow daylight to enter. I was impressed by the architecture, as I often was by various buildings I saw throughout the world, and have never understood why British architects have been slow to capitalize on good foreign ideas.

We had come to Genoa to load vehicles of a South African regiment for transportation to Durban and Captain Ffoulkes called us to his cabin on the evening of Thursday, 23 May, to inform us that he had invited a dozen officers of the regiment for dinner the following evening. He asked us to make the South Africans feel welcome and said that all the drinks were being paid for by himself, Mr Quayle and Mr Turner. The majority who came were captains, there were two or three majors and a colonel; and there was a great deal of drinking. The evening was rounded off by a number of our officers going ashore with them to the 'Ragno d'Oro' (Golden Spider) nightclub. The hospitality shown to the South Africans was generously reciprocated. They put a small truck, with bench seats, at our disposal on the Saturday and invited us to a dance at their mess in the evening.

Genoa is in the centre of the Italian Riviera and the South Africans had suggested that we used the truck to go along the coast to Rapallo. An Italian driver was provided and when he came on board in the morning, Mr Quayle told him to take his instructions from me. As nobody was ready and a few were suffering the effects of the previous evening, I told him to come back at 1.30pm. You would have thought that there would have been fierce competition for a seat on the small truck, but this was not the case and it was able to accommodate all who wanted to go. Tony, Bill Harrison, Peter Pratt and I were among the few.

The trip proved most enjoyable with wonderful views from the high and tortuous coastal road. We were in Rapallo and Portofino and saw Santa Margherita far below us as we passed. It was too cold for the rest of the party, but Tony and I swam at Portofino before we went into a café where we were served by a shy waitress and a man played softly for us on his mandolin.

The dance at the South African Officers' Mess in the evening proved equally enjoyable. A tall slim English-type major took me under his wing and introduced me to a beautiful young blond Italian Contessa who, he said, "looks as if she would, but won't"! I sat beside the Contessa and an older lady and had started to ask the Contessa to dance when Peter Pratt intervened so that she danced with him. Manners then dictated that I should ask her older companion. She knew no English, but was fluent in Spanish as she had lived in the Argentine and we tried to communicate in that language. When I thought that she said that she was 21, I laughed and she became irate until I eventually grasped that it was her daughter who was 21!

Our trip along the Riviera on the Saturday had been made in glorious sunshine, but, on the Sunday morning, when the truck arrived to take us to Lake Como, the rain was coming down in sheets. We waited, hoping that the rain would cease, but it rained heavily the whole day so that the trip was cancelled.

We sailed at 11am on Wednesday, 29 May with eleven passengers on board; ten South African soldiers, including a Lieutenant, and a young Dutch girl who was engaged to a Captain in the regiment. As we moved from the quay, the girl's father, whose home was in Florence, waved her goodbye. No doubt he had a heavy heart and wondered when he would see his daughter again as the age of cheap air travel had not yet arrived.

*The *Samnesse* did not have a passenger certificate so that our passengers signed-on as supernumeraries. One 22-year-old soldier gave a Genoan address and an Italian wife as his next of kin. Most of the soldiers were big Afrikaners who spoke English with a guttural accent, but Lt. Hammond was a small, quietly spoken, man who could have been mistaken for an Englishman.

11   ENROUTE TO SOUTH AFRICA

We were to call at Haifa in Palestine for fuel oil. The weather was favourable and I saw Etna again as we passed through the Strait of Messina.

We were nearing Haifa, when, on the evening of Sunday, 2 June, Captain Ffoulkes brought our girl passenger to my cabin and introduced us by asking if I could get the Italian news for her on the radio. I did this and after she had, dutifully, listened to the news, Elena van praag, who was 25 and signed her surname in low case letters, sat talking to me in my cabin as she did during many subsequent evenings on the long haul to Durban. In the letter which I posted home from Haifa, I wrote "What a change this is from the wartime racket! Here I am sitting in my own cabin. I can switch on the radio and hear the programme while sitting at my desk. I have a nice looking girl spending the evening talking to me and best of all - I go to bed and can sleep for a solid 8 or 9 hours. Gee whiz!"

Elena was a tall, pleasant, slim, fair-haired girl. She had a sister in South Africa and I believe that she was going to live with her sister until her fiancé, a South African Army Captain, was able to return home and they would be married. She was interested in photography and had a movie camera plus a Leica which took 'still' pictures. Her movie camera had cost 140,000 lire (£155 10/-), an enormous sum in those days, and she gave me several black and white prints of the Matterhorn, Monte Bianco (Mont Blanc) and the Dolomites which had been taken when she and her fiancé were on holiday together. But most of her pictures were in colour which was then a medium beyond the pocket of most of us. Elena read palms and, looking at mine, she said that I had a long lifeline. When I asked her, "How long?", she said, "Not more than 90."

Captain Ffoulkes, whose cabin was on the same (bridge) deck, was always around and one evening he came in and offered us sweets and then looked 'hard' at me when he saw the grin on my face. On another evening he came and positively stared at me when he thought that Elena was staying too late. 9pm seemed to be his deadline and he later lectured me on the Blue Funnel rule that no passengers were to be admitted into officers' cabins! Ffoulkes was already a fatherly friend and I had gone for a walk with him in Genoa. But he was a fusspot and everything had to be done his way. He was always around us and Tony and I referred, not unkindly, to him as Shorty. Elena spoke excellent English with a Dutch accent and I have always remembered the phrase "You know dit (that)?" which she constantly used. I also remember that she rounded on me one evening when I mentioned the 'Ragno d'Oro'. I had heard of the place only from Tony and, according to Elena, it had a bad reputation and was not nice.

The auto-alarm had broken down on the way to Genoa and we had had it repaired when in port. It broke down again on Monday, 3 June, but this time I was relieved when we located the fault in a small screw which had worked loose. During the evening we passed HMS *Ajax*, of *Graf Spee*/River Plate fame, and exchanged words with her on the signalling lamp.

Although the passage to Haifa was good, our passengers were all off-colour when we temporarily encountered a swell. We dropped anchor in Haifa harbour at 0030 hours on Tuesday, 4 June.

Palestine was a troubled place with conflict between Arab and Jew and with the British in-between, trying to maintain the peace, but a target for both factions. The seeds of the conflict had been sown during the First World War when Palestine was part of the Ottoman Empire and when Britain succeeded in enlisting the help of the Arabs against the Turks, by promising them independence after the war. But she had not kept her promise and, by the Balfour Declaration of 1917, had given her support for a 'national home for the Jewish people' in Palestine. In 1920, the League of Nations gave Britain the mandate to rule Palestine and this was why there was a British presence in the country with our Forces and Palestine Police left to 'hold the baby'. The Royal Navy had the job of patrolling the Eastern Mediterranean in order to prevent ships from landing Jews illegally in Palestine. The Jews were desperate to get out of European countries, where they had suffered so much under the Nazis, to begin a new life in a new Jewish homeland.

Haifa, the principal port of Palestine and with Mount Carmel as its background, looked lovely in the sunshine, but we had no opportunity to go ashore until we went alongside to fuel at 9pm on the Wednesday. During Tuesday and Wednesday the ship lay at anchor in the lovely harbour, but some of us enjoyed this by swimming 'over the side'. Few, however, took the opportunity because the beautifully clear water was teeming with jellyfish and, even with of a man posted above the gangway to warn us of their proximity, Mr Turner was stung.

It was shortly after 10 o'clock on Wednesday evening when Tony and I went into town. On leaving the docks, we passed brightly lit cafés, where Arabs sat chatting over drinks, and walked into the town centre. All the shops, cinemas, etc. were closed by then: British military police and British Palestine Police patrolled the streets and native police occupied strategically placed sentry boxes. Rolls of barbed wire lay at the sides of the streets in readiness to cordon them off if trouble should erupt and now and again an armoured car went by with a Tommy set high behind a Bren gun. I recalled the many posters displayed throughout the UK at the time, encouraging young men to join the Palestine Police with the offer of '£20 a month and all found'. As far as I was concerned, the job was not worth 'all the tea in China'!

As Tony and I re-entered the docks, we passed a group of our crew heading for the town. And, in the group was Butler, our cabin steward, who looked so scruffy that we would have been ashamed to have been associated with him ashore. Butler, aged 38, was from Liverpool and a most interesting man with whom we had many discussions. The Merchant Service carried many clever men on the 'lower deck' and I believe that Butler was one of them. But, Butler, who, no doubt, had been brought up in disadvantaged circumstances, had chosen the easier way of sneering at all those above him rather than strive to improve his own position. Tony was, justifiably, proud of his rise from the 'lower deck', but made the mistake of allowing this to be generally known. The people you 'leave behind' are, generally, resentful and Godwin, the Captain's Tiger and, in my opinion not nearly as clever a man as Butler, tried to ingratiate himself with me by suggestive remarks about Tony. I gave Godwin short shrift and considered him senior to Butler because he was ingratiating and more reliable.

Having bunkered during the night, we were out in the harbour again by 9.30am on Thursday. The oil came by pipeline from the Kirkuk field in northern Iraq and was refined in a refinery in Haifa which had been built just prior to the war. When Iraq, Egypt, Syria and Jordan went to war against the newly proclaimed State of Israel in 1948, the pipeline was severed.

We sailed for Port Said at 5pm on Thursday, 6 June. I regretted that I had not seen much of Haifa and Mr Turner told me that, on a previous visit, he had visited Bethlehem and Nazareth from the port. Our mail went free, as it had done from Greece and Italy, and, later, from Egypt. Our letters were stamped either 'Field Post Office' or 'Maritime Mail' and sometimes had 'O.A.S'. (On Active Service) written on them. I considered this somewhat ironical when we had had to pay for letters posted in Algeria during the war.

We arrived in Port Said at 8am on Friday and entered the port, as was normal, flying the yellow Q (quarantine) flag from a halyard on the bridge. The flag signified that we had a clean bill of health, but that no unauthorised person could come on board before the port medical officer had granted us pratique. I met the Port Medical Officer, answered several questions and signed a declaration that we had no infectious disease on board. And, as soon as he granted pratique, and the Q flag began to descent, the bumboat men raced up the gangway and spread their wares out on deck. Along with them came a barber and a gulli-gulli man who performed magic tricks such as bringing white mice from his sleeve. There were also others who would make purchases for us in the town. George Brydges was in my cabin when an Arab tried to sell me a watch and when George suggested that there might be nothing under the pretty face, the Arab turned on him with venom. George put his face close to that of the Arab. "Are you threatening me?" he quietly and menacingly asked and the man immediately became ingratiating.

We spent the day at anchor, just yards from Sultan Hussein Quay, the main thoroughfare on which the renowned store of Simon Artz was located, and took on board the bow light and generator which were necessary for night transit of the Canal. We also took on board an Arab and his coble so that he could tie the ship up to bollards on the Canal's western side when a ship, from the south, was due to pass. And, with a pilot on board, we entered the Canal in the late afternoon. We had to tie up twice in the Canal, exited about 3am, and dropped anchor in Suez Bay at some distance from Port Tewfik.

The Agent came out in a launch from Tewfik and I met him at the gangway to receive and give him mail. Holt's officers were not paid overtime, but our salaries were higher than the minimum laid down by the National Maritime Board and nobody cared what I was doing at any particular time as long as I did the job. Incidentally, agents, who were almost exclusively British in the ports which we visited, had to turn out at any hour of the day or night when a ship arrived or sailed. And, on many occasions they were under pressure as time is money and a ship must never be delayed without due cause. Some forty years after I was on the *Samnesse*, I frequently played golf with George Simpson, who had been employed by Mansfield, Blue Funnel's Agent in Singapore, and he remembered Ffoulkes as a pompous master whom he did not like. I couldn't help smiling; Ffoulkes could be pompous when he chose to be and George, himself a pleasant man, rightly deduced that Ffoulkes had the almost inherent sailor's disdain for shore wallahs!

Having discharged the bow light and generator, we weighed anchor about 4.30am and proceeded south, through the Gulf of Suez, towards the Red Sea.

We had changed into tropical uniform on the passage to Haifa, but it was not uncomfortably hot until we reached the Red Sea. Most of us wore khaki, but, in compliance with Captain Ffoulkes' order, we changed into whites and wore black ties at dinner. But it was ridiculous to wear ties in such heat so that we tore them off as we left the saloon and, seeing our resentment, Ffoulkes relented and the practice was discontinued. The Red Sea was not at its hottest, but it was hot enough and the all-steel Liberty Ship retained the heat until the early morning. Intake fans fitted in Genoa, and the slow moving fans in our cabins, brought little relief.

The heat of the Red Sea was nothing to that which we experienced after passing through Hell Gates and entered the Gulf of Aden and it was in the Gulf that we heard the *Antilocus* on the air. It was the practice to contact another Blue Funnel ship when we heard her and to exchange greetings and the names of the R/Os. And the name of the 2nd Sparks of the *Antilocus* was Neville Caro. It was a moment I enjoyed. Caro had been 2nd Sparks on the *Samite* and *Samforth* when I had been 3rd. We had spent over two years together, but had more or less just tolerated each other. And here he was, still No.2 when I was No.1. He was 'on the (Morse) key' and, typically, made no reference to knowing me. I told Tony to send Bon Voyage and Caro reciprocated. We heard the *Samforth* (MYQN) the following day. She was bound for Aden, from Fremantle, and I asked if Blundell, who had been 5th Engineer with me on her previous voyage, were on board. He was and was now 4th Engineer. I sent my regards and later received his reciprocation.

Also in the Gulf, a P&O passenger ship passed close to us on her way to the Far East and called us by signal lamp. Bill Clow, our 3rd Mate during the coasting voyage, was her officer-on-watch and sent his felicitations to all who knew him.

It was the season of the southwest monsoon. We were in bad weather for a whole week after rounding Guardafui and our passengers were not seen for several days. The ship rolled slowly over to port until you thought she was going right over, then there was a momentary pause before she swung rapidly to starboard. All Liberty Ships behaved in this manner, but having been on the *Samite* and *Samforth*, I was well used to it. In the region of the Equator, we were joined by the albatross and their smaller cohorts. The flock, looking for scraps of food from the ship, flew alongside us during the day and rested on board at night.

As we proceeded down the coast of East Africa, we ran neck and neck with the Liberty Ship *Samcebu* and became friendly with her R/Os although we never saw the ship. She was bound for Montevideo and still had three R/Os on board as she had been away for ten months and had been to Canada and the west coast of Australia. Her R/Os were from England, Wales and Ireland and we kept in constant touch. And, when her 3rd Sparks signed off, he identified himself by sending 'shamrock'. On the morning of Tuesday, 25 June, the *Samcebu* asked if we would accept [11]Ocean Letters for posting in Durban. I said to have them ready for the afternoon watch, but they came back in the afternoon and said to cancel the request as they were putting in at Capetown with a sick seaman.

As supernumeraries were 'paid' at the nominal rate of 1/- (5p) a month, it was unnecessary to provide them with wages accounts when they signed off. But, as we neared Durban, Captain Ffoulkes composed a humorous account as a souvenir for Elena and I typed it out on the legal form. An item on the credit side read 'for darning the Captain's socks' and another 'for darning the Captain's other pair of socks'. And Elena was left with a balance of one tickey! (The South African three-penny piece which was replaced by the five-cent coin in 1961.) Regrettably, Elena's South African fiancé reneged on his promise to marry her so that it was fortunate that she had a sister in the country.

I do not remember where Elena was accommodated, but Captain Ffoulkes, on this occasion, did not ask Tony to give up his cabin. I suspect she was given the cabin on the main deck which was kept for the use of a pilot but, because she was the only woman on board, Ffoulkes allowed her to use his toilet and shower room which lay between Tony's cabin and the wireless room. The soldiers were accommodated in what was euphemistically called the 'hospital' and the rooms beside it which had previously been occupied by DEMS gunners. This accommodation had the disadvantage of being over the propeller with its associated noise, but, fortunately, we were fully loaded. When we were light ship and she pitched, her screw raced when it came out of the water and the noise was deafening.

As we neared Durban, I worked out what each man would have in his

---

[11] An Ocean Letter was a message sent from one ship to another for posting from a port of call and the charge was 5/- (25p) for the first 20 words.

account on arrival and, a day or two before we arrived, sent round the usual sheet asking what each wished to 'draw'. The total came to £325 and some, as I had come to expect, wanted to 'draw' more than they, after the deduction of allotments, steward's account (purchases on board), etc. had at their disposal. Only one or two did this and I was never sure if it were because they didn't keep a check on their spending or if they were 'trying me on'.

When we were within range of Durbanradio (ZSD), we sent our ETA and, although we were not aware of it on this first visit, this information was published in the shipping section of the Daily News the following day. On later occasions when we were heading for Durban, and when many of the lads had girlfriends in the port, we were constantly asked if we had contacted Durban. The information in the 'paper acted as a free telegram and alerted their girlfriends to expect them!

We changed back into blue uniform on Tuesday, 25 June and docked in Durban on Thursday the 27th. Apart from the hour in Haifa, I had not been ashore for a month, but was in no way discontented. During the passage, I had read, inter alia, a bit of the Old Testament, 'Three Men in a Boat' by Jerome K. Jerome and the [12] Wide World Magazine. And dhobying, of course, was a constant chore.

On arrival, I received fourteen letters. And as my father had been with the 9th Worcesters when they were carried to Durban by HMT *Tahiti* in 1917, for transhipment to India, and had often spoken of the place and the hospitality he had received, I was particularly keen to see Durban.

---

[12] The Wide World Magazine was a favourite of mine and I became a member of "The Wide World Brotherhood" by sending, I think, 'half-a-dollar' (2/6d or 12½p) to the Magazine. In return, I was given a membership certificate, signed by the Editor, and the lapel badge by which other 'brothers' might recognise me. None ever did and I never saw anyone else wearing the badge although my membership number was 14,196. The WWM contained only true-life adventures and sold throughout the world. Sadly, due to lack of support, it went out of existence many years ago.

12   DURBAN, NATAL

Durban is situated on the eastern side of land-locked Natal Bay and the entrance to the port, between the almost 200 feet high promontory of the Bluff, on the west, and the low spit of the Point, on the east, is only 450 feet wide. We tied up at the Point and within walking distance of the town centre.

It was the Port Medical Officer who first informed me of the Durban July Handicap; South Africa's premier horse race which takes place annually on the first Saturday in July. In 1946, the 'Great Winter Meeting' at Durban Turf Club's racecourse at Greyville at the foot of the Berea, extended over the three days, 6, 10 and 13 July. The July Handicap race is held on the first day of the Meeting and corresponds somewhat with our Derby in that the whole country takes an interest.

Although we arrived nine days before the race, Durban was already in a state of excitement at the prospect of the event and the ship was soon caught up in the fever. A sweepstake was held on board and we all chipped in 2 bob (2/- or 10p) in the hope that we would draw a horse. I drew a blank, but Ernest Pennington, the 2nd Mate, drew [13]Lochiel and he and I decided to go along to see it run.

Ernest and I ate at the same table in the saloon and were discussing the race over lunch on the day of the meeting when D.C. Dumbill, the saloon steward, overheard our conversation and asked Ernest to put 12/- (60p) on Lochiel for him. Ernest was irritated by the request, but, being a kindly man, didn't have the heart to refuse and accepted the bet from the steward.

It seemed that all Durban was attending the meeting and the next day's newspaper reported that an estimated 40,000, including the Governor-General and a party from Government House, were present and that all the enclosures were packed and parking space at a premium. It also reported that "The weather was fine and warm, the course and enclosures being in excellent condition, although the going was on the hard side owing to the absence of rain." (I have an idea that Durban received no rain for something like 9 months that year.)

We took one of the special trams labelled Race Course and arrived at an

---

[13] The correct spelling and not as 'Locheil' in Scotland.

entrance by which Asians and Cape Coloureds (people of mixed blood) were allowed to enter. Almost all those present were Asian and we found ourselves in a section reserved for them when we entered the course. We were walking to the entrance gates when a well-dressed Indian approached and thrust tickets in my face. I have never been much of a businessman, but the man was so overbearing that I asked what he wanted for them. Apparently, he had changed his mind about going in and wanted the same price as they were selling for at the entrance so that I asked why I should buy his tickets when I could buy them at the same price at the gate. He seemed taken aback by this but, when we moved towards the gate, he let me have them at a reduced price.

I had come only to see the race and experience the atmosphere, but, like Dumbill, Ernest wanted to place a bet on Lochiel and I stood beside him at the tote as he gave his order to the clerk. Ernest wished to place only a small bet on the horse plus, of course, the 12/- bet for the steward. When the busy clerk informed him that the minimum bet accepted at the tote was 10/- (50p and not an insignificant sum in those days), he reluctantly concurred and the clerk issued a 10/- ticket. Ernest then immediately said, "And twelve", meaning an additional bet of 12/- on the same horse, but, because bets at the tote were accepted only in multiples of 10, the clerk issued a 10/- ticket for horse No.12 which was Desert Rat! Ernest, of course, protested, but the deed was done. The clerk refused to change the ticket and Ernest was stuck with a bet on the 20 to 1 'outsider'.

We witnessed a race or two before the main event of the July Handicap was run at about 3.30. The race was over one mile two and a half furlongs and, prior to it, the horses were paraded and applauded by the spectators. St. Pauls, at 11 to 1, romped home in 2 minutes 10 seconds, two and a quarter lengths ahead of Moscow. Lochiel was a close third and Desert Rat somewhere among the 'also rans' so that Ernest was left kicking himself for the misunderstanding which had sent his 10 bob down the drain.

As the odds on Lochiel were 12 to 1, Ernest collected 27/- (£1.35p) for the place bet and, being the gentleman he was, handed over the money to Dumbill without mentioning what his obligation to the steward had cost him. But I thought that Dumbill should know of the 2nd Mate's sacrifice and, when I told him, he looked sorry before adding that it was a pity that his other 2 bob hadn't also been on the horse. The idea of sharing the spoils never crossed his mind and perhaps it was fortunate that Lochiel didn't come in first.

There was no shortage of anything in Durban's shops, but, for us, everything was expensive. The suit which I badly needed cost the astronomical sum of £16 and this just about cleaned me out.

All our city centres are now almost deserted in the evenings, but Durban was the first place I encountered where this was the case and I was struck by the difference between the busy town during the day and the quiet town in the evening which seemed unnatural. Cinemas were, of course, open in the evenings and, as the citizens dressed-up to attend performances, the atmosphere was akin to that of a theatre. Seats were booked ahead of a performance and a decent seat cost 3/3d (16.25p). Performances began at 8pm with an interval for refreshments at 8.30. The Playhouse Theatre was unique in that it had a ceiling which resembled the sky on a clear night and the Southern Cross could be identified. The less palatial cinemas were called bioscopes; a seat cost 1/- (5p) and included in the price was a glass of lemonade or a cup of tea served on a folding ledge attached to the seat in front.

Tony and I went on a coach tour to the Valley of a Thousand Hills which was a Zulu Reserve and Europeans were liable to a fine of £25 or three months imprisonment if they entered without a permit. The round trip was 75 miles and I found it difficult to keep awake as we drove through the dried-up undulating countryside before arriving at a Zulu kraal. The people were dressed as their ancestors had dressed and appeared to be living in much the same, primitive way. We were in the Chief's beehive hut, saw how mealies (ears of maize) were ground on stone querns, to make porridge and beer, and how spearheads were beaten into shape over open fires. Spears and other items were offered for sale and the highlight of the visit was when the boys and girls of the tribe danced for us. They were obviously enjoying themselves and everybody laughed when they pushed a boy, of only about four years of age, in front of the dancing line and he danced brandishing his little spear in the air. The youngsters ran after our coach as we left and we threw coins to them out of the windows.

It may now seem ludicrous, but it did not enter my head that, in a black man's country, it was strange that there were only white people on the beach. There was no mention of apartheid in these days, but black people were excluded from all the public places and only those employed as house servants and performing menial tasks for the whites were seen in town. There were, of course, the rickshaw 'boys' (of any age) in their colourful headdresses who made their living from tourists.

According to the 1936 census, the population of Natal (Europeans, Coloureds, Natives and Asiatics) was 1,946,468 of which only 190,549 were European. The following is a quote from the Durban Visitors' Guide of 1946: "Domestic Servants at Durban are usually Bantu peoples, chiefly Zulus, though, in a lesser degree, Natal Indians are employed, and, in some households European domestics are preferred. Kitchen and houseboys, waiters and cooks are paid from £3 upwards per month and nursemaids from £2 per month. In small households one boy or woman usually suffices and gives excellent service. Accommodation and food are provided by the employer. There are no standard rates of pay, nor set hours."

I was on the beach one afternoon, when an anxious dad gave his son a good 'hiding' when he came out of the water. He had warned the boy not to go out too far because of the danger of sharks, but the boy had ignored his instruction. Although it was winter in the Southern Hemisphere, it was a holiday season and the beach was always crowded.

I made use of the Merchant Navy Officers' Memorial Club at 17 Gardiner Street. At the South African Officers' Mess in Genoa, the major had said of the Contessa, "she looks as if she would, but, won't". At the Club, an engineer said of a girl, "she looks as if she wouldn't, but does."! Although the dances, held every Saturday night, were rather subdued affairs, I enjoyed them and often danced with the same girl. But, when I asked her for a 'date', she pleasantly refused. Drinks were served at the small tables at which we sat and I always indulged in a couple of Van der Hums.

A heavily built elderly gentleman spoke to me on the quay one morning and asked if I could get him a loaf of bread, baked on the ship. According to him, you couldn't get decent bread in Durban. Ffoulkes granted the request and I introduced the man when he came on board. He had been an officer with Blue Funnel and annoyed Ffoulkes by criticising the quality of the ships (Liberties) which they now operated. But, 30 years later, I heard Ffoulkes voice the same opinion.

E. Knight, the 2nd Cook/Baker, had become ill and on Tuesday, 9 July, Captain Ffoulkes and I went with him to the Shipping Office where he was paid-off and landed into hospital. After a dance at the Mission that evening, five of us were invited by two sisters, one of whom was in the WRNS, to their beautiful house on the Berea for coffee.

I went to the Missions to Seamen, in Wellington Road, Point, much more than I did to the MNOMC. Under a young padre, all those involved in the running of the Mission did all that they could to make merchant seamen welcome. The girls who came to the Mission were all clean-looking friendly girls who conversed to each other in a patois of Afrikaans when they did not want us to know what they were saying. Picnics and football matches between ships were also organised for us. Letters posted at the Mission went free and arrived home stamped 'Certified As Ship's Mail Posted Through The Missions To Seamen, Durban' and 'On Naval Service. Official Free. Africa Station.' An airmail letter given to the ship's agent, Wm. Cotts & Co. Ltd., cost 1/3d (6.25p).

Sunday 7 July was a Sports Day at the Mission with all ships in the port competing. The [14]*Arundel Castle* came first and the *Samnesse* second. When there was another Sports Day the following Sunday, we again came second with the *City of Bristol* first. Although I did not attend these events, I have an excellent photograph of some of those who did, along with girls of the Mission. It is a picture of a happy group, but I think that there was an inner happiness in all of us as we were living in a post-war euphoria. I had taken my father on board the *Samtucky* in Dundee during my last leave and she came into Durban during our stay.

I sent a food parcel home from the Mission where we had only to select a numbered parcel, pay for it and they did the rest. Parcels took about three weeks to reach the UK and postage cost almost as much as the contents. In a local shop, I bought tins of custard powder, gooseberry jam and pineapple chunks, four jellies in powder form, two packets of currants and a packet of assorted dried fruits. Such items seem inconsequential today, but were still luxuries in post-war Britain.

The Governor-General was to visit the Mission and the printed invitations, delivered on board, read as follows: "THE CHAIRMAN AND COMMITTEE REQUEST THE PLEASURE OF YOUR COMPANY ON THE OCCASION OF A VISIT BY HIS EXCELLENCY, THE GOVERNOR-GENERAL, THE RT. HON. G. B. VAN ZYL, P.C., TO THE HEADQUARTERS OF THE MISSIONS TO SEAMEN, DURBAN, ON TUESDAY, 16th JULY, 1946, AT 4 P.M." Each ship was asked to send six men to be part of the Guard of Honour.

Although we were enjoying ourselves, the world news was depressing.

---

[14] Union-Castle ships arrived every Tuesday at 7am and departed on Thursdays at 5pm.

The USSR, our wartime ally, was now our enemy and, although a second war 'to end all wars' had just ended, atom bomb tests were being conducted. A letter from my parents informed me that David Cathro was home and had paid them a visit. He was now out of the RAF and back working in Henry's office. In my reply to the letter, I wrote, "Must find out what Henry's are going to pay him, for I've been thinking it over a lot lately and don't think it would be wise to throw up a [15]£32-10/- a month job for a £12 a month one. If I have to stay on at sea I'll have to study hard though as I certainly don't intend staying in this racket all my life. It's difficult to know just what to do."

Anticipating returning to work in the Dundee office, I had visited the factory of The Durban Bag Co. (Pty) Ltd., a subsidiary of A & S Henry, the day after our arrival. The factory was at Jacobs, on the outskirts of the town, and the area was in marked contrast to that of central Durban as there were many black people walking about and the roads were unpaved. Rather naively, I expected that, coming from Dundee, I would receive a special welcome, but this was not the case. The staff were friendly enough, but I left with the feeling that the visit was a mistake.

Having discharged our cargo, we moved to the coaling station at the Bluff so that we had to make the short crossing on the ferry before taking a trolley bus into town from the Point terminus. The ferryboat ran every fifteen minutes and the return fare was 6d (2½p). Two of our wet batteries had proved faulty and when a young electrician brought replacements on board, he vehemently expressed his view that black people were [16]inferior. "I know", he said, "that a black man and a white woman can walk together in London, but if I saw this here, I would do something about it."

When I visited the whaling station at the Bluff, I innocently asked a man as to the large protrusion on one of the dead whales. He looked at me quizzically before saying, "That's its penis."!

On the morning of Saturday, 20 July, we were ready for sea, but moved only to an anchorage in the harbour as two firemen were missing. One of

---

[15] On 6 July, when I completed three years at sea, my salary had been increased from £18 to £21-10/- a month; the £10 a month 'war bonus' and the £1 purser's bonus made up the rest. And this was a good salary in 1946.

[16] At Edinburgh University, thirteen years later, a Singhalese student expressed the same opinion about the Tamils. "That's what the whites said about you in South Africa," I said. "I know", he replied, "but they *are* inferior."

them turned up, but the other, 32-year-old J Howarth, was listed as a deserter. When I made an inventory of the clothing he left behind in the cabin which he shared with three other men, I felt nauseated by the unnecessary squalor in which he had lived.

As we lay at anchor that Saturday night, with the enticing lights of Durban twinkling from the shore, I regretted being unable to attend the dance at the Officers' Club.

With our cargo of coal, we sailed for Port Said on the morning of Sunday, 21 July, 1946.

Postscript: Vasco da Gama was the first European captain to round the Cape of Good Hope which had previously been reached by his fellow countryman Bartholomew Dias in 1488. This was in 1497 and when, on Christmas Day, he sighted the Bluff, at what is now Durban, he named the territory Terra Natalis (Land of Birth) from which the name Natal is derived. Da Gama, however, did not land and it was not until 1824 that a British settlement was established in the bay. It was named Port Natal, but renamed D'Urban in 1835 in honour of Sir Benjamin D'Urban who was then governor of Cape Colony.

13 PORT SAID VIA ADEN

The radio messages we sent and received were generally to and from the ship's agents at the various ports-of-call, but it may have been on this passage north that one, originating in the UK, was transmitted to us from our Area Station, Radio Ceylon. As reception on the short-wave frequency was very bad, Tony managed to get only isolated words on the first transmission. At the second transmission, six hours later, we both tried to receive it, but it was not until the third that we finally got it – a message to Ernest, saying that his father had died. I don't know how he came to know about the receipt of the radio telegram, but Ffoulkes later came to my cabin to enquire as to its content and, aware of our commitment to secrecy, I said, "I'm sorry, sir. It was a private message for Mr Pennington". Ffoulkes stalked off in anger, but returned shortly afterwards and, still angry, said, "I'm master of this ship and should know the contents of all messages sent and received". "Well, sir", I replied, "the message informed Mr Pennington that his father has died". But, on receiving the information, to which, as master, he was perfectly entitled, Ffoulkes appeared to regret that he had intruded.

Dressed in khaki shirt and shorts, Mr Turner appeared at my door and challenged me to a game of medicine ball. I had never heard of the game, but he had a heavy elliptical ball in his hands and said that he would show me how to play. We played over a rope strung across No.3 hatch and, although he at first led by 5 to nil, I, with youth on my side and half his age, won by 6 to 5.

Every day during the passage north, I washed an article of clothing. I also scrubbed bulkhead panels clean, as even with portholes closed and ventilators stopped up during loading, the dust was everywhere. And I never look at the Chamber's Etymological Dictionary and the Philips' Record Atlas, which I still have, without remembering that I had to blow the dust off them on the *Samnesse*.

The weather was more kind than it had been on the passage south, but although it was uncomfortably warm by Wednesday, 31 July, the wind blew strongly and a high sea ran throughout the night so that waves were coming as high as my cabin on the bridge deck. As I had no alarm clock, I always asked Mr Turner to waken me and when he did this at 7am on Thursday morning, he laughed at finding me sleeping with both portholes open. Later that day, we rounded Guardafui and high cliffs were visible to port.

We were calling at Aden to bunker and I was up at 5am on Saturday, 3 August to be ready to meet the PMO and the [17]Agent on arrival and to notify the local radio station that we were entering the port. There were no docks/berthing facilities at Aden and it was 8am before we dropped anchor among the other ships anchored off Steamer Point. The oil pipes from the shore terminated at buoys. We connected up to them and oil began flowing into ours bunkers. I gave the ship's mail to the Agent, but he had nothing for us. By 6pm, we had taken 850 tons of oil on board and sailed for Suez.

In the Gulf of Suez, Mr Turner called me to the bridge to see Mount Sinai through his binoculars and we anchored in Suez Bay at 5.30am on Friday, 9 August. And, having taken a pilot on board, commenced the journey through the Canal about 10am. In order to change pilots we anchored for a time off Ismailia and a number of us took the opportunity to swim over the side. Because of the danger from sharks, we could not swim in Aden harbour or in Suez Bay, but I often wondered why they didn't use the Canal.

We anchored on the eastern side of Port Said harbour at 11pm and, as I had met port officials at both ends of the Canal, it had been a long day. Port Said had no docking facilities and we joined other anchored ships tied up, stern to the breakwater.

The dirty and noisy business of discharging our coal began the following morning and I soon regretted that I had spent so much time scrubbing the bulkheads of my cabin as coal dust was again everywhere. In the holds, a gang of Arabs shovelled the coal into buckets which were swung over the side by the ship's winches and their contents dropped into barges.

On Saturday I spent a couple of hours swimming in the harbour and Ernest and I went into town in the evening. A fast motor launch went round all the ships collecting passengers, but as it was expensive, we elected to engage the services of an Arab in his rowing boat. The Arab was not a young man and, with his bare feet on one of the thwarts, it took him what seemed an interminable time to row us to the shore. He then asked for the same fare charged by the operators of the motor launch and, when I pointed this out, he said "Motor boat very easy, rowing very hard." He did not understand economics, but he was right and we grudgingly paid what he asked. We had intended going to the pictures, but, as we had missed the

---

[17] Blue Funnel's Agent in Aden was Luke, Thomas and Co., but we always referred to an Agent's representative who came on board as 'the Agent'.

first house and the second did not begin until 9.30pm, decided to give the cinema a miss.

The town was very busy and we were continually pestered by Arabs trying to sell us whips, blackjacks, fezzes, nuts, newspapers, 'dirty' books and postcards, etc. We were approached by unsavoury individuals asking, "You want jiggy-jig?" while others wanted to clean our well-polished shoes. As to the other vendors; we said we didn't like nuts, had read all the newspapers or couldn't read!

The shops were open and there were many British servicemen in the streets. I spent 30/- on swimming trunks, Johnson's fine grain developer, a Spanish grammar and views of Port Tewfik and Suez. The Egyptian £1 was roughly equivalent to the British £1. By 9.30pm we had seen enough of Port Said and were rowed back to the ship. The town looked lovely from the sea, but we were left with no desire to visit it again.

Three of us hired a coble for the day. We rowed about the harbour, went swimming over the side and when we saw that we were directly in the path of a liner exiting the Canal, we hastily climbed on board and rowed frantically out of its way. The weather was lovely. We entered the coble shortly after breakfast and although, by lunchtime, I felt that I had already had enough of the sun, I did not want to miss the fun and went out in the coble again until 4pm. It was after dinner that I realised how foolish I'd been. I was severely sunburned and spent a painful night. The skin came up in large watery blisters and my hands were blistered from rowing. It was a salutary lesson and my back still bears the marks which were left.

We had been a fireman short and without a 2nd Cook since Durban and J. Shaw and C.W. Parker had been sent out from home to fill these posts. Mr Steadman, our 3rd Engineer, hit his foot with a 28lb hammer and was discharged into hospital on 15 August. Bill Harrison was promoted to 3rd and Mr Walker to 4th.

A small group of us stood on the bridge to watch the new *Stentor* (GMTC) pass slowly to enter the Canal on her way to the Far East. When I expressed admiration for the ship and said that I'd like to be on board her, Mr Turner said what were to prove prophetic words, "You won't say that when you're on one of these fast ships and have to work all the hours."

With the decks hosed down to rid the ship of coal dust, we sailed for Genoa at about 5pm on Sunday, 18 August, to carry another load of South

African army vehicles to Durban. And, after a week of living in a dirty and noisy atmosphere, it was a relief to enter the Mediterranean.

14   RETURN TO GENOA

The passage to Genoa, in relatively calm seas and under blue skies, was absolutely glorious. Just before entering the Strait of Messina at 8am one lovely clear morning, we saw Etna again and then passed so close to Messina that we could make out people by the naked eye. Later the same day, smoking Stromboli was so near on our starboard side that I could see deep ruts made by lava from the volcano and the houses of the people who lived on northwest side of that small and unstable island.

When I listened to the BBC programme 'Mediterranean Merry-Go-Round' and the question "Where is Sardinia?" was asked, we not far from it. On the evening of 23 August, Monte Cristo lay to starboard and the 2nd Mate's chit told us that [18]clocks were being advanced by nineteen minutes that night. This put us on the same time as Italy and the UK and we arrived in Genoa at 6.42am on Saturday, 24 August.

We were met with such unusual neglect on arrival in Genoa that we instinctively felt there was something wrong. And when the agent eventually arrived, I was summoned to Ffoulkes' quarters. Ffoulkes was angry. "We shouldn't be here," he shouted. "We should have gone into Naples and Naples has been trying to get us all night." This was one of the worst experiences which a radio officer could suffer, but the words *all night* gave the solution. The Agent had sent the telegram late the previous evening and Naples had been calling us during the night when only the auto-alarm kept watch. He should have known the hours we kept, but offered no apology and said that we were to leave for Naples in the evening to load for the UK. I slit open the letter to my parents which I had ready for posting and said that they could expect to see me in three or four weeks time. But Naples was cancelled and it was back to Durban.

The speaker in Captain Ffoulkes' cabin, connected to the receiver in the chart room, 'packed up' and he had Tony replace it with the one in the officers' saloon. I deduced that Ffoulkes knew that the officers would only moan, but that the crew would be up in arms if the speaker were taken

---

[18] A change in time was always made at midnight. Clocks were advanced when proceeding east, retarded if proceeding west, and we always arrived in port on local time. The 2nd Mate sent these chits to all departments, but a daily one to the wireless room giving our noon position, course, speed and distance covered since the previous noon, as this information could prove vital in an emergency.

from their mess. I repaired the offending speaker, put it up in the saloon, and he was left with a speaker which was painted differently from the rest of his cabin!

I bought a second hand Gewironar, folding, camera, with an f/6.3 lens. Included in the price of £5 were a leather case and a film. There was no shortage of Italian films and I bought twelve of the 120 size and printing paper.

As the shops were well stocked with items almost unattainable in the UK and clothes unrationed, this could have led me to believe that the Italians were better off than the victorious British. But, although at 900 lire to the £1, food seemed cheap to us, there was still the daily gathering of women and children on the quay begging and, as before, Ffoulkes had bread baked for them. Fruit was plentiful with a kilo of grapes costing only about 7d (3p).

A general election had been in the offing during our previous visit and the buildings in Ferrani Square had been smothered in red posters of the Communist Party. The posters had now gone, but large painted slogans remained so that I wondered at the intelligence of people who could deface their beautiful city in such a manner.

Sugar and cigarettes were in short supply and, anticipating our return to Genoa, some of the crew had bought these and other items in Durban to sell in the port. When we had stopped momentarily on entering the harbour, a rowing boat approached the ship and its occupants called out asking if we had anything to sell. I was unaware of the situation until I heard a bellow from Ffoulkes and saw him storming down to the main deck from the bridge. Dead against the black market, he shouted at the boatmen to clear off. And, not having paid for the goods they had received, they rowed away laughing while our black-marketeers stood grimly by.

Almost all of us sold cigarettes and even the armed Italian guards on the ship were in on the racket. One afternoon, when I knew that a 'deal' was going on in the 3rd Mate's cabin, I hammered on the door for a bit of fun. This brought the desired result. Accompanied by the sound of muted voices, there was a great deal of scuffling behind the closed door. And it was a greatly relieved George Brydges who opened the door and saw that it was 'only me'. Cigarettes were plentiful on the black market and stands throughout the city displayed packets of twenty US cigarettes at 7 or 8/- (35/40p). Our 'duty free' Players cost only 1/6d (7½p) for a tin of 50.

Tony, George and I had an excellent spaghetti-based meal in a lovely restaurant where the waiters told us they had served on such fine ships as the "Rex", "Conte di Savoia" and "Conte Verde". There were many counterfeit notes in circulation. They were difficult to recognise although printed on thinner inferior paper than the real thing and George, who had only counterfeit notes, handed them to me as his share of the bill. Although I didn't like this, I gave the lot to the waiter. We walked decorously through the restaurant, descended the steps, and 'took off' when we reached the street!

The weather was glorious until the morning of Friday, 30 August, when there was a violent thunderstorm. I hoped that it would continue to delay our loading, which had gone on day and night since the Tuesday, and let us have Saturday in port. But the sky cleared by 9am and loading was completed that day.

Eleven South African soldiers embarked shortly after breakfast the following morning. I signed them on as Supernumerary Deckhands and had difficulty with addresses such as Potchefstroom in the Transvaal. This time three soldiers gave Italian wives as their next of kin. On his first voyage to sea, 20-year-old R Blundell had arrived from the UK to make up our complement of engineers.

I had received no mail in Genoa and surmised that it had gone to Naples. On my last day ashore, I had bought an alarm clock which saved me having to ask Mr Turner to call me in the mornings.

We sailed for Durban at 1.10pm on Saturday, 31 August. Precise times were entered in the Official Log Book and I often noted them in my diary.

15   SECOND VISIT TO DURBAN

The sea was moderately rough on our departure so that our passengers skipped a meal or two. But this didn't last long and we were soon sailing in good weather. We changed back into tropical uniform and, eager to try out my 'new' camera, I took pictures of Stromboli, when we again passed within a mile of it.

We arrived in Port Said harbour at 4.32am on Friday and anchored near Sultan Hussein Quay. The missing mail did not appear and the Agent brought only one or two letters and a few newspapers from home: I got a Sunday Post, a Peoples Journal and the August issue of the Signal, the magazine of the ROU (Radio Officers' Union). The routine already described was followed before we weighed anchor at 7.56am, transited the Canal and anchored briefly in Suez Bay where the Agent, devoid of mail, made a hasty visit. When we sailed at 7.35pm it was a relief to hear the engines going full away as we headed into the Gulf of Suez.

Our radio watch-keeping times altered when we entered the Red Sea. My 2-hour morning watch had previously begun at 0800 hours GMT, but now I began the watch at 0400 hours GMT. This meant that, during our passage through the Red Sea, I began my watch at somewhere between 6 and 7am ship's time. A few of the fellows took badly with the heat, but I felt great because I could limit my time in the sun and was not subjected to the intense heat which others had to suffer.

On the evening of Sunday, 8 September, I was called to the bridge during the 4 to 8 watch. An American Liberty Ship had called us on the lamp and the Morse was too fast for Mr Turner. The Yank had come from Archangel and was bound for Vladivostock. We talked for ages with Mr Turner telling me to ask questions about Archangel, etc. Captain Ffoulkes was also on the bridge and when the Yank asked who was on the lamp and I told him, he said "Skipper here". Surprised by this, I turned to Captain Ffoulkes and Mr Turner and said, "Do you know who's on that lamp? It's the Skipper." Captain Ffoulkes wasn't deaf, but said "Who?" in such a way that I immediately realised that I should have said "The Captain". But the Yank had said "Skipper" and when I, precociously, repeated the word, Ffoulkes remained silent!

During a morning watch, I contacted the homeward bound *Laomedon* (GRQF). I was corresponding with Eric Cameron, who had been 3rd Engineer with me on the *Samforth* so that I knew he was on board and we exchanged greetings. I then asked the radio officer to make a continuous signal so that I could make an attempt at calibrating our D/F (Direction Finder). He obliged, but within minutes, our D/F fused. Later in the day, Tony and I pored over the circuit diagram and thought that we had found the fault until we attempted to calibrate the device against another passing ship when the fuse blew again. It was back to the circuit diagram and the fault was found.

We were barely over this crisis when we found that one of our receivers would not tune into stations. We speedily rectified this but, on the morning of Wednesday, 11 September, ships told us that only clicks were coming from our transmitter. Hearing of our predicament, an R/O on another Sam Boat called us up and said he had experienced similar trouble and suggested a remedy. I appreciated, but did not take his advice and did nothing. The problem disappeared and we came to the conclusion that the fault arose due to the aerial down-lead being soaked and causing an earth when the decks were being washed down every morning.

The Apostles lay to port at 6pm on Tuesday and we were off Perim by 8am the following morning. And, having negotiated the Strait of Bab el Mandeb into the Gulf of Aden, we turned eastward along the dry and inhospitable coast of Arabia. There was no relief from the heat and the pen kept slipping from my fingers when I wrote. By 4.30pm the 'Barren Rocks of Aden' were in sight. We were calling to bunker and anchored beside an oil pipe terminal off Steamer Point at 6.20pm. Bunkering went on throughout the night and we sailed at 5.59am the next day, Friday the 13th of September, 1946.

We had to notify local radio stations when we were entering or leaving port, but, when I tried to contact Adenradio (ZNR) as we moved slowly out of the harbour, the transmitter refused to function. This was serious and Tony and I pored over the circuit diagram from early morning until late at night until I was able to report to Captain Ffoulkes, on Tuesday, that the transmitter was again working.

The intense heat was reduced, but the sea became rough once we rounded Cape Guardafui. The night of Thursday 19/Friday 20 was particularly bad. A heavy swell commenced about 1am and the ship rolled heavily. A receiving aerial came down and the main aerial grounded against a stay. I was hanging on in my bunk and sleeping only fitfully, when Ffoulkes burst in saying, "You'd better have a look at the wireless room." Although locked, the top drawer of the filing cabinet, which stood at the port bulkhead, had shot through the open door and there were papers all over the alleyway. As I've already mentioned, Liberty ships rolled frighteningly and a few rolled right over when their cargo shifted. The *Samkey* and two other Liberties disappeared without trace and the *Leicester* (ex-*Samesk*) had a narrow escape after she listed to 70°.

We arrived at Durban a day or so earlier than we had expected and at about 3pm on the afternoon of Wednesday, 25 September. The pilot boat came out to us, the pilot leapt onto the gangway, and he had us alongside by 4 o'clock. But the PMO didn't arrive to 'clear' the ship so that we had to gaze down in frustration at the Agent who stood on the quay holding the bag which we hoped contained mail. Also on the quay were the parents of one of our passengers whose home was in Durban. And, when the doctor did 'clear' the ship, the bulk of our mail was still missing. The Agent brought some cash, but, as this fell far short of the amount I required from him, I was able to provide each man with only a fraction of the sum he had requested. Nevertheless, this allowed us enough spending money to go ashore and, in the evening, Mr Turner and I went to the Metro to see Esther Williams and Van Johnson in 'Easy to Wed'; the first film we had seen in over two months.

I had been on the *Samforth*, in Lourenço Marques, in May, 1945, when a letter arrived from A & S Henry in Dundee asking if I intended to apply for reinstatement when I was "released from the Service" and I had answered in the affirmative. But now that I had a permanent job with Blue Funnel, I was doubtful if I wanted to return when I was much better paid and enjoying life at sea. I had spent many hours wrestling with the problem, but it was solved for me when I received a letter in Durban. The firm had been "beaten by numbers" so that they could take back only those who were with them before 4th September, 1939 and I had joined them four weeks after that date. But I was in no way downhearted. Without knowing it, they had made the difficult decision for me and, during my leave, I had seen an ex-RAF Squadron Leader reduced to sitting again on his high stool!

When I went to the Mission to send another food parcel home, the man at the counter said that the Post Office had 'phoned that very day to say that, without warning, the Government had stopped the sending of all parcels. But he later called me over to the counter again to complete the necessary form. Parcels already ordered were allowed to go and he would slip my one in with those. But, within 48 hours, the Government order was rescinded.

As we had been away for over four months, the books in our 'library' had been well read. I boarded a nearby ship to ask if they would like to exchange 'libraries' and, when they agreed, packed the wooden box provided and carried it to the other ship. And, believe me, the other ship had to be nearby, as it was a struggle to carry the heavy load from and to the *Samnesse*.

With all cargo out, the ship moved from Shed Q to Maydon Wharf where she had to wait until a ship vacated the graving dock to allow her in to have her bottom scraped.

At an Officers' Club dance, I made a date with Mavis Kenyon whom I had met there during our previous visit and we went to the Playhouse and then for a meal. We arranged to meet again although I told her that our departure date was uncertain and we may have sailed by then. And when we did sail that day, I had no regrets because I was skint!

I was gradually replacing my stolen clothes and the Wren we had met on our first visit had procured white shirts and shorts for me from naval stores. She was a PO and now the only remaining Wren in Durban. She came down to see us off and, with a white handkerchief in each hand, signalled to us in semaphore until she was only a spot in the distance. The 'Lady in White', who had sung to the troopships as they left Durban during the war, had already passed into history, but our 'Lady in Blue' was equally appreciated.

J. Moister, fireman, was discharged due to illness and Duncan Gilchirst, from Blackridge in West Lothian who was a deserter from the *Nea Hellas*, replaced him before we sailed on Thursday, 3 October - bound for Lourenço Marques (now Maputo) to load coal for Massawa and Djibouti. It was only a short run and we berthed at 2pm the following day.

With Laurie Morgan (right), Antwerp.

'Taffy' Davies, lieutenants, driver and me with local family, Hasselt village.

At the Parthenon, Athens.

Mission sports, Durban, July, 1946

Bunkering a coal-burner, Port Said.

Rowing us ashore, Port Said.

IN RANGE OF DURBAN

APPROXIMATE positions of ships in range of Durban radio at noon to-day:—

Inward: Bradburn, Fort Chambly (unreported); Manoeran, 80 S.W.; Samarovsk, 610 N.E.; Tibia, 280 N.E.

Outward: Atlantian (unreported); For Glenora, 230 E.; Selma Victory (unreported); Towerhill, 190 N.E.

Various: Britissh Bombardier, 115 E.N.E.; Cromarty, 250 N.E.; Tiradentes, 525 N.E.

The following ships were in port at noon to-day:

Shed A: White Falcon.
Shed A-B: Grainton.
Shed B-C: City of Calcutta.
Shed C: Explorer.
Shed D: Chas. W. Stiles.
Shed E: Rio Colorado.
Shed F: Atlantico.
Shed G: Okeanos.
Shed G-H: Fort Bourbon.
Shed L: K. Rapanos.
Shed M: Gazana.
Shed N: Demonocus.
Shed N Ext.: Sondra.
Shed O: City of Carlisle.
Shed O-P: Fantee.
Shed P: Hickory Broom.
Shed Q: Samnesse.
Shed R: Agulhas.

BLUFF:
Beaton Park, Templeyard, Octon Valley, Fort Slave, Fort Wrigley.

MAYDON WHARF:
H.M.S.A.S. Barbrake, Whalers, Pipina, S.A.N.F. Le Norwegian II, Mareschal Gallieni, Greenwich, Whalers, Robin Locksley.

GRAVING DOCK:
Two whalers, Harbour Craft.

Arrivals Yesterday: Ocean Valley from New York; Tower Hill from Buenos Aires; Explorer from East Coast for Liverpool; White Falcon from U.S.A.; Samnesse from Genoa for Lourenco Marques.

Arrivals To Noon To-day: City of Calcutta from East Coast for Canada and U.S.A.; Grainton from Buenos Aires; Fort Wrigley from Aden for Lagos.

Expected To-morrow: Manoeran from Gulf ports for U.S.A.; Carrier Pigeon from New York for East Coast; Fort Chambly; Bradburn, Tibia, Kolsnaren.

Departures Yesterday: Nahoon, Fort Glenora, City of Madras, Cecile Mapleson, Selma Victory, Samfinn, Good Hope Castle, Sandown Castle, Tower Hill.

Departures To-morrow: Templeyard, Ocean Valley, Fort Wrigley, White Falcon, City of Calcutta.

Daily News, Durban, 26 September, 1946

At the Lido, Massawa.

Massawa

Native quarter, Massawa.

Station on Massawa-Asmara line.

Corsa Italia, Asmara.

The main square, Djibouti.

Djibouti

Native quarter, Steamer Point, Aden.

Samnesse, Dar-es-Salaam.

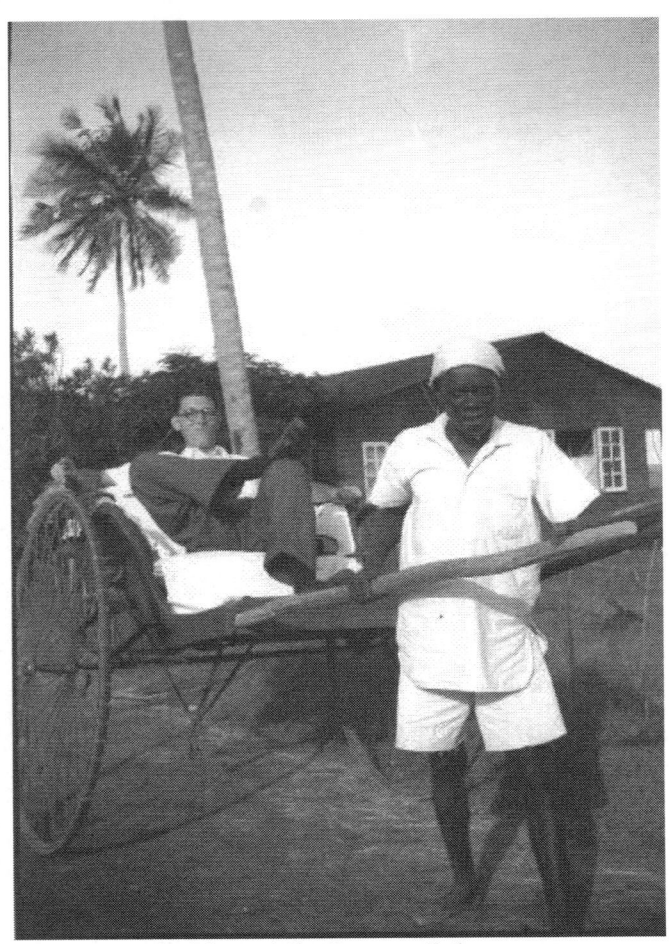

Pukka sahib, Dar-es-Salaam.

Discharging coal, Dar-es-Salaam.

Discharging coal, Dar-es-Salaam.

Captain A.J. Ffoulkes, Dar-es-Salaam.

Swimming party, Tanga, Christmas 1946.

Samnesse entering Durban, 5 January, 1947.

In the Wireless Room.

"Are you busy just now Mr. Wilkinson?"

Placed anonymously on our notice board.

Ernest and me, St Mark's Square, Venice.

The Waterfront, Venice

Allied Military Currency

Tripoli

Main street, Bône.

With Captain Ffoulkes, Birkenhead, 1975

16 LOURENCO MARQUES

Although the transmitter had continued to function since we had effected the repair, it had been behaving erratically so that I requested that a radio engineer have a look at it. We were at anchor in the bay on the Saturday when Pieter Van Dijk found that the fault lay in the power transformer and took it ashore to have it rewound in the railway workshops. And when Mr Van Dijk invited Tony and me to spend the night at his house, we gratefully accepted.

Mrs Van Dijk was a good-looking blonde who appeared to be younger than her husband, whom I put to be in his forties, and the couple, who were Dutch and not Afrikaners, lived in a beautiful house in an elevated position overlooking the lovely bay. With native help, they enjoyed a high standard of living. We went to a cinema in the evening and when I stood beside Mrs Van Dijk in the queue waiting to get in to see a Perry Como film, she remarked to me on the appearance of another European lady in the queue. And I knew from the remark that she was fishing for a compliment on her own appearance.

Tony and I returned to the ship the following forenoon and went to see Laurel and Hardy in 'Bonnie Scotland' in the evening. I had seen the film about ten years previously in the Kinnaird Cinema in Dundee, but it stood seeing again and it was an experience to sit in a black audience who laughed as much as the Dundee audience had done. Although there were only whites in the Durban cinemas, this was not the case in Portuguese East Africa/Mozambique. The sound track was in English with Portuguese subtitles on the screen.

We were invited back to spend the Wednesday night at the Van Dijks and again gratefully accepted as the ship was now coaling and it was a relief to escape the noise and the coal dust. The Van Dijks had two sons who were 'away at school' in, I think, Southern Rhodesia (now Zimbabwe) and Tony and I occupied their room. When we rose late in the morning, Mr Van Dyke had gone off on some job and Mrs Van Dyke barged into our room a couple of times so that I struggled behind the door to get on my trousers before she barged in again. I found her behaviour embarrassing, but Tony found it hilarious! Before returning to the ship in the afternoon, we spent some time with her in the sitting room while she knitted.

It was an irate Captain Ffoulkes who stormed into my cabin brandishing the account which had been presented to him for the repair of the transformer. "Look at this," he shouted, "£100!" It was an enormous amount and he obviously held me responsible. "And," he went on, "What right had you to get the Company to pay for your boat trips ashore?" and he held the copies of the chits I had signed when travelling in a motorboat from our anchorage in the bay. I had no defence and remained silent while he continued his diatribe. But it was the Ministry of Transport would be footing the bill and I doubt if they even noticed it. On a later occasion when I had ordered a few stores, Ffoulkes, in the presence of the Chief Engineer, jokingly referred to stringent pre-war days when a Blue Funnel torch had been a candle!

Suffering from polyneuritis, B. Edwards, Fireman, was discharged and J. Barnard, a 21-year-old from Benoni in the Transvaal, signed on as his replacement.

Again in filthy state, so that I gave the ship's name in a letter home as the 'Somemess', we sailed for Massawa at 2am on Saturday, 12 October, 1946. We had received no mail in the port and I had had only 2 Peoples Journals and 9 letters since 10 August.

17   THE ADOPTION OF THE SAMNESSE

During our August stay in Port Said, Captain Ffoulkes had received a letter from The British Ship Adoption Society asking if he would agree to have the ship 'adopted' by a school. This meant that he and others on the ship would write to a school and that the pupils would write to us. Ffoulkes had shown me his reply and the contents of the letter certainly surprised me. He said that he had already heard of the Society and had always thought that the idea behind it was to give young boys a false impression of sea life - that it was a great life seeing foreign ports, etc. without mentioning the bad aspects of the life. He went on to say that the Merchant Service generally attracted the wrong type of boy, that it could do with some decent lads, and condemned shipowners for not keeping their part of the bargain as they were interested only in cheap labour. I never thought that a Master, and a Blue Funnel one at that, would have the courage to write in such a vein and wondered what Holts would have made of it had they known. But Ffoulkes, a loyal servant of Blue Funnel, no doubt had other shipowners in mind and, in spite of his remarks, agreed to have the ship 'adopted'. The Society had asked if he would like to nominate a particular school and he opted for Barnstaple Girls' Grammar School which his wife had attended. I gave no thought to it at the time, but it is likely that he chose the Girls' School, not only because his wife had gone there, but because he did not wish to be responsible for boys embarking on a career in the Merchant Service. But, once he had made up his mind to be 'adopted', Ffoulkes embraced the idea with enthusiasm and badgered all the officers to write to the School. But he came up against a brick wall. The general view was that they had nothing to write about and Mr Turner expressed his opinion that, "If they want to know anything about the sea, ask my wife."! But I liked the idea of ship adoption so that I supported Ffoulkes.

Confirmation of our link with the School had arrived in Durban, but it was after we sailed from Lourenço Marques that he asked me to write to the School explaining the work of the radio department. The weather was excellent when I sat in the sun on the small open bridge deck during the afternoon of Monday, 21 October and wrote the long letter which I subsequently typed and handed to him. I thought it excellent although he said only that it was 'quite good'! But I could see from what he later wrote to the School, that he had learned from what I had written, just as I learned from his letters to the School which he had me type.

I have a copy of the British Ship Adoption Society's 1946 booklet explaining the Society's origin, aims and work. Under the section addressed to schools, it states: "........... Heads and staffs will appreciate that the captain and officers on board - their counterparts in the ship - welcome, and indeed expect, a note from them to show that their interest is not confined to the scholars.........." But, although I wrote to pupils over a period of six months, no staff member ever communicated with me and I didn't even receive an acknowledgment of my letter describing the work of the radio department. And, as the girls who subsequently wrote to me were only 12 and 13 years old, the contents of that letter was well over their heads.

Bearing in mind the resistance met by Ffoulkes, the contents of some of the letters I received from pupils and my later experience as a teacher, I find some of the contents of the BSAS' booklet hilarious. In the section addressed to Masters, it states "A ship will receive the greatest value from the scheme if interest in the correspondence *is spread as quickly as possible among the officers and men* (italics as in booklet). Some members of the crew will naturally be more apt than others at taking a share in the correspondence, but experience has shown that a master who succeeds in spreading the interest is helping on the good work of making his ship a "happy" ship." The *Samnesse* was a happy ship, but our link to Barnstaple Girls' Grammar School was more likely to have had an adverse effect on that condition than otherwise! All letters to and from schools were sent en bloc, in large envelopes, via the BSAS' office in London and as soon as a consignment of letters arrived on board, Ffoulkes distributed them with an enthusiasm which was not reciprocated by us. Regarded as a positive menace, he stamped round the accommodation happily and literally throwing letters at us to answer as we sat reading our mail. Even although I was willing to co-operate, I resented this plus the fact that he seemed to take it for granted that I type all his letters to the School.

In the same section of the booklet directed at masters it says "Masters may find it useful to get the ship's agent to arrange voluntary visits for the crew (particularly junior officers), to towns and villages and to factories and plants ashore, e.g., power stations, cotton factories, museums, mines, growing crops. For example, an eye-witness's account of the process of pressing cotton or tapping rubber would be welcomed in a school. ...." This suggestion almost doubles me up with laughter. There were people representing the National Union of Teachers, the Educational Institute of Scotland (of which I am now a Life Member) and Inspectors of Schools on the Society's Committee of Management, but whoever wrote such rubbish could well have profited from a spell at sea in the Merchant Service. He certainly was astute enough to mention junior officers who were the most vulnerable, but the thought of crew members giving up valuable drinking time to traipse round a factory or museum....! Alternatively, the writer may have thought that a master would give men time off work to see how cotton was processed although the shipowners' representatives on the Committee could have put him straight on that score. They would have soon have 'educated' any master whose ship remained in port longer than necessary in the name of education with a capital E!

I still have the letters of three girls who wrote to me. All wrote well for their age, with clear writing and good spelling, but now in their late sixties, the ladies would laugh at some of the things they wrote.

Hazel Jenkin, who lived in the village of Landkey Newland, was my only regular correspondent and, by the time she wrote her letter of 5 March, 1947, she was addressing me as Ian. Hazel wrote ".......Could you tell me please who keeps the boat clean? I expect that there is more than one person who cleans the ship. Isn't there? Is Captain Ffoulkes a stern captain or an easy captain?...........P.S. Thank-you very much for the photograph of the 'Samnesse'. Good sailing!"

In her letter of 17 February, 1947, Judith Francis wrote "........Today we were going to have singing in the hall and we went there; there was a stream of water dripping from the ceiling, a pipe had burst so we have been sent back to our formroom and I have taken a job of writing a letter to you. .... When Captain Ffoulkes wrote his last letter he told us that on board ship you have six cats and a monkey. You are lucky. I love cats and I all ready have five of my own and when I told my Aunty about the monkey she said that she wished it was her's for she has always wanted a monkey. ......My uncle used to be a sailor, I think he was a Lieutenant or something like that........"

Judith mentioned that Miss Rosser was her geography teacher and I seem to remember that this lady came from the Mumbles, near Swansea. This has stuck in my mind because the Mumbles lifeboat was lost with all hands when attempting to rescue the crew of the *Samtampa* in a 70 mph gale on the night of 23/24 April, 1947. The *Samtampa* had anchored, but her anchors had dragged and she was driven on to the rocks at Sker Point, near Porthcawl, where she broke up. All 39 of her crew perished in addition to the eight gallant lifeboat men.

On 26 February, 1947, Margaret Sweeney wrote ".........To be a Radio

Officer do you have to know geometry, or do you only have to know all about wireless? (I would have settled for knowing all about wireless!).....Do you take it in turns to be in the control room by hours or days?......On the wireless I listen to, Dick Barton, William, Variety Bandbox, The Carol Levis Show, Family Favourites, and nearly every programme after 4 o'clock......It is ten minutes to nine by the clock, so I must finish for now......."

The days of my association with the British Ship Adoption Society were already far behind me when, in June 1961, I was browsing in the library of Kirkcaldy High School, where I was completing my final spell of teaching practice. Always looking for books about the sea, I came across 'Seafarers, Ships & Cargoes' and could scarcely contain my excitement when I found that it was a compilation of letters/articles to schools and contained one from Ffoulkes which I had typed and another from Mr Sawle, the Chief Steward, which Ffoulkes had had me knock into shape. I don't think that Ffoulkes ever wrote to individual pupils as I did, but only general letters to the School. All his letters describing life at sea, navigation, cyclones, etc. were interesting, but, in the first part of the letter in 'Seafarers, Ships & Cargoes', he displays his own fine character.

SHIP ROUTINE
S.S. "Samnesse"

Dear School,

With the Comoro Islands behind us we shall see no more land until we approach the extreme north-east corner of Africa, Cape Guardafui, about 1,500 miles away. Nothing to see but sea and sky, occasionally a school of porpoises, perhaps a whale or a shark or two, and shoals of flying fish. Now that we have the open sea around and before us, we will return to a discussion of your ship. It is nearly 10 p.m., and we are steaming into a dark but starry night. In these latitudes the stars always seem larger and brighter than they do in England, except, perhaps, on an occasional frosty, winter night. I love those still, frosty English winter nights when you can almost hear the stars crackle as they twinkle. The ship is gliding along with hardly any roll or movement except the throb of the engines the ship's beating heart.

On the bridge walks the Third Officer, who has charge of the watch from 8 p.m. until midnight. He must be ever alert. On him more than anyone else depends the safety of the ship. "Eternal vigilance is the price of

Admiralty." I don't know who said that but it is very true. At the bow the look out does his two-hour trick, reporting to the bridge by telephone every half-hour, or whenever he sees anything. On the bridge the man at the wheel also takes a trick of two hours. His job is not hard but it needs his attention. In this fine weather he should never be more than two degrees off his course. In the radio room a radio officer "keeps a look out with his ears". In a few minutes he will go off watch, and then for a few hours the only wireless watch will be kept by an automatic alarm. This is operated by an [19]S.O.S. signal which may come through. One sailor walks the deck below the bridge ready for anything that may be required. In the engine-room the Fourth Engineer Officer is in charge and with him he has one "greaser", who does all the oiling of engines; in the stokehold one fireman attends the boilers. That does not sound many people, but as we burn oil the fireman has little to do but watch his jets to see they don't go out.

That is the working organization of the ship. I am just below the bridge if I am needed. In a few minutes I shall be writing in the "Night Order Book" any orders I wish to give the officers for the night. Then I go to bed, too. And while we sleep the ship steams on into the night, each of us trusting others with our lives, as they in their turn trust us. This necessity to do one's duty and trust others to do theirs is just as great in every walk of life. Society cannot function to the full, and give us all the safety and happiness we should have, unless everyone pulls his weight and does his duty...............

The British Ship Adoption Society was formed in 1936 and, in 1946, there were some 1200 ships and over 800 schools participating in the movement. Every member school was expected to pay an annual fee of £3.3s. Fees paid by local education authorities qualified for a 50% grant from the Ministry of Education and shipping companies contributed according to the number of ships and tonnage owned.

With the decline in British shipping, the Seafarers' Education Service and the Marine Society amalgamated and, in 1976, absorbed what was left of the work of the BSAS. In 1988, the term Ship Adoption was changed to that of Sea Lines as today's links are made between schools and individual seafarers.

---

[19] The auto-alarm was actually activated by the auto-alarm signal which was sent before the SOS. This consisted of twelve 4-second dashes with a space of one second between each, but it required only four consecutive correctly spaced dashes to set bells ringing.

During the passage north, Ernest allowed me to steer the ship during his afternoon watch. With the quartermaster standing idly by, I had the wheel for an hour and, although the weather was fine with only a moderate sea running, I did not find it easy to maintain the course as a mere touch of the wheel altered it.

Incidentally, boat drills were regularly held when the ship was at sea and recorded in the Official Log Book as shown in the following example:

Date.   Crew mustered at Boat Stations wearing life jackets.
Emergency appliances test and found to be in good condition.
Nos. 3 & 4 boats swung outboard.
Fire drill carried out fore and aft/amidships/in accommodation/for'ard.

18   MASSAWA

After a pleasant run from Lourenço Marques, we docked in the Red Sea port of Massawa at 4.26pm on the afternoon of Thursday, 24 October. The main port of Eritrea, it had been occupied by the Italians since 1885 and in, 1946, 10% of the town's 20000 population were Italian. But, since their defeat in 1941, Eritrea had been under British military occupation.

The discharging of our coal began about two hours after we docked and as usual all our portholes and ventilators had to be closed/blocked up to prevent coal dust entering our cabins. We were thankful when work stopped at midnight so that we could open the portholes to obtain some relief from the heat while we slept, but after that first night discharging went on day and night and we slept fitfully in our hot and airless cabins. According to the 1944 Handbook published by the British Ministry of Information, the climate of Massawa is "barely supportable from June to October....". But this, of course, does not take into account living on an all-steel ship with portholes and ventilators closed to keep out coal dust! The Lido was a lovely place to escape to and particularly so in the cool of the evening when lights played on the water and we could sip drinks under a starry sky.

Asmara, the capital of Eritrea, was just over seventy miles away and I went there with Mr Turner. We rose at 5.30am and George made us breakfast of poached egg on toast before we caught the 7 o'clock train, which was called a rail car and resembled a single deck tram. The first part of the journey was through barren and dried up countryside, but as the train, which ran on a single track and was diesel driven, wound its way higher and higher over the hills towards Asmara, the views became superb. Almost all the passengers were Italian and we were enjoying the journey when we were startled by a sudden commotion. It took us a few seconds to realize what was happening; the train had run into a swarm of locusts and the passengers were slamming the windows shut to prevent them entering. Cold drinks were served on the train and, as we neared Asmara which is 8,000 feet above sea level, the air became pleasantly cooler and even somewhat chilly.

Asmara was a modern Italian city with a pleasant climate very different from that of Massawa. Its temperature is usually 25°F lower than that of Massawa and it receives 21" of rain while Massawa receives only 9; next to nothing as moisture evaporates rapidly in the intense heat of the coastal plain. We arrived at about 10.45am and had only a short time at our disposal as we were booked to return on the 2.30pm bus. The reason for this was that Ffoulkes had suggested to Mr Turner that we should return by bus in daylight in order to see the countryside and as the journey took approximately 4 hours, we would be back in Massawa before dark. I was against this and would like to have stayed longer, but Maurice agreed with Ffoulkes and I deferred to his seniority. When we subsequently found that the road ran alongside the rail track, I knew that I had been right. Ffoulkes, of course, meant well and it was he who had the Agent procure our return tickets which we had to collect from Gellatly Hankey's office in Asmara.

Our first objective was to get the tickets and a British military policeman directed us to the office. We were hungry and, on leaving the office, dined at the Savoy where the meal was not cheap but excellent: soup with rolls and butter, a pasty dish, steak with potatoes and spinach, fruit salad and ice cream, coffee and white wine. It was 20 minutes before we could rise from our chairs!

We wanted to see the town and hired a gharri, which could hold three people, for an hour. It was a wise move. We saw the town in comfort and felt like lords as we drove along the wide and beautiful Corso Italia; a world removed from the hot and dirty "Samnesse". Our return journey to Massawa by bus was not as comfortable as the train journey but, because the bus was cheaper, we travelled with more of the natives.

Massawa was pleasant in the mornings and one morning I met a young Geordie 2nd Engineer who took me to a small Italian café where we had drinks served by the wife of the owner. As we sat in the cool café, the engineer told me that although he was now somewhat fed-up with his job on a small vessel which traded only in the Red Sea, he had taken it because it had offered him a senior position at an early age.

I was tramping the streets with my camera when I met three of our fireman out for a stroll. When I asked them if they had seen anything worth photographing, they took me down an alley and into a courtyard in the native quarter. Some young girls were having their hair done by older women sitting on chairs, a lady in national dress was strumming on an odd shaped stringed instrument and men sat at benches drinking beer. I asked if I might take a picture, but as soon as I brought my camera from its case, the girls fled. A woman of about 30, however, was keen to have her picture taken with a boy of 15 and, when she stood beside the boy, I had her move a little distance to the side so that I should get a view of the people at the back. I took the lady's address in order to send her a copy, but, due to the heat, the emulsion on the film disappeared when I was developing it.

From the courtyard, we struck further into the native quarter and down narrow streets with primitive native shops. When we came to a mosque, I was keen on entering, but a very black fellow approached me and said, in English, that I couldn't do this. He announced proudly that he too was *English* as he was from Aden, then a British Colony. The mosque had open sides so that I could see men prostrated towards Mecca although most seemed to be sleeping on the floor.

I got to know the crewmembers quite well. Every evening the steward provided sandwiches for our supper and either Tony or I descended to their mess, two decks below, to obtain hot water for our cocoa from the urn. There were always several sailors or firemen sitting there chatting and they were always ready with banter. Our sandwiches, incidentally, came on a plate covered by another plate in an attempt to protect them from cockroaches, but it was seldom, if ever, lifted without several of the insects scampering away. If we had been too fastidious we would never have eaten any supper.

The remainder of our cargo was to be discharged in Djibouti and it appeared likely that, from there, we would head for a port in Southern Africa to load more coal. As to where we would take that coal was a matter of speculation, but rumour had it that it was to be either the West Coast of Africa or the Plate.

Captain D.W. Dix, who worked for Gellatly, Hankey, wanted a passage to South Africa for his wife and 4-year-old daughter, Denise. The problem was, of course, where they could be accommodated and Tony's double-berth cabin was the obvious target. But, with the benefit of previous experience, Ffoulkes put the problem to Tony and requested that he move into the pilot's cabin on the main deck as otherwise Mrs Dix and her daughter would have to be berthed in the spartan hospital at the stern. Put that way, Tony had no choice. He agreed to the proposal and generously refused payment for his inconvenience offered by Captain Dix. Mrs Dix and her daughter were to join the ship in Djibouti and I believe this was for two reasons. One was that our destination was uncertain as, even when we arrived in Djibouti, it seemed that there was the possibility of us returning to Massawa for a cargo of salt. The other was to avoid the uncomfortable experience of being on board when we were discharging coal in Djibouti as they joined only the day before we sailed from that port. And I seem to remember their object of going to South Africa was to escape the heat of Massawa for a spell.

We sailed for Djibouti, via Aden to bunker, at 7.16am on Wednesday, 30 October. We had received no mail in Lourenço Marques and, as it was a repeat performance in Massawa, we hoped that letters would be waiting for us in Aden.

Postscript: Eritrea continued to be administered by Britain until 1952 when the United Nations Organization linked it with Ethiopia against the wishes of the Eritrean people. An armed struggle ensued and continued after Haile Selassie's Government was overthrown and replaced by the Marxist-Leninist regime of Lt. Col. Mengistu, in 1974. It was not until the Mengistu Government was deposed that independence was won in 1993 and during the 30 years of conflict, Massawa suffered great destruction. Independence has not, however, resulted in a country at peace. For fear of attack by bandits, today's tourists are advised not to deviate from the road between Massawa and Asmara on which Maurice Turner and I travelled.

19   DJIBOUTI VIA ADEN

After the 400-mile run from Massawa, we anchored in Aden harbour at 6.15am on Friday, 1 November and at long last received mail. But although I got 14 letters and a postcard, some of the fellows complained that much of their mail was still missing and the middies reported that some letters sent by their parents had been returned to them. We were, of course, tramping so that destinations were always uncertain, but this did not excuse such an inefficient mail service now that the war was over.

As I had never previously had the opportunity to go ashore in Aden, I jumped at the chance when Captain Ffoulkes asked me if I'd like to go. He was not going himself, but wanted some (bought) pictures of the place for the School. Tony came with me, a launch took us to Steamer Point and we tramped round the place with me taking snapshots with my 'new' second-hand camera. In a subsequent letter home, I said "What a joint! I've seen the place now and never want that privilege again." But, two years' later when on the *Atreus*, I saw a great deal of interest in that barren place.

Mr McNeill, our 2nd Engineer, who had developed some medical complaint, was transferred to the homeward bound *Atreus* while R.B. Cable, from the same ship, replaced him. Unlike Mr McNeill, Mr Cable had only his 2nd Engineer's Certificate and had, no doubt, been promoted because he agreed to the transfer. He was only 25 and one day as he sat in the saloon, Ernest remarked to me that it did not seem right that such a young man should sport three gold bands on his uniform. I saw his point of view as he, a 28-year-old 2nd Mate who had been at sea since before the war, had a salary of £29 a month while Mr Cable, who had gone to sea years later, had a salary of £34.5/-.

It was only a short distance to Djibouti and we anchored, a considerable distance from the shore, at 9.12am the following day. The setting, in the unrelenting sunshine, was lovely, but the heat was excessive and with our portholes and ventilators again closed to keep out the coal dust, it was, to say the least, extremely uncomfortable. And as only our own winches were used to discharge the coal into lighters, the process was so slow that it took 17 days to off-load the remainder of our cargo.

Gellatly, Hankey, again our Agent, provided a launch to take me to the town to get money for the crew on the afternoon of our arrival. Bill Harrison came with me and we were surprised and disappointed at the primitiveness of the place. There were no made-up roads and pavements and only stone kerbs separated the one from the other. And as it was the afternoon siesta, the few shops and unattractive-looking cafés were closed and the town almost deserted. Nevertheless, there was some attractiveness about the town due to several fine buildings and palms and other trees which lined the streets.

In Djibouti, I answered the letters I had received in Aden and my letter to my parents was headed S.S. 'Samcollier' whereas, after coaling in Lourenço Marques, I had headed one 'Somemess'. My father and mother had expected me to be despondent at been rejected by Henrys, but I wrote that I was not the least sorry about this and hadn't the slightest desire to get another clerk's job. I had set my sights on getting my 1st Class PMG and, as Dundee Wireless College had now closed, I would have to go to the college in [20]Edinburgh. A fellow I had met in Lourenço Marques had told me that this was a municipal college, that the tuition was excellent and that the fees were much lower than those charged by private institutions.

My parents had asked me about David Cathro and I had received a letter from him telling of his return to Henry's. He had been given the choice of remaining in the Dundee office at £350 pa or going to work in the office of E. Carr & Sons (a subsidiary of Henrys) in London at £450 pa. He had told them that, after 4½ years in the RAF, he valued home comforts and that an additional £100 was not sufficient inducement to give them up or even to cover the additional cost of living in London. David had said that he had given me this information in confidence and didn't want it to be passed on to John Noble to whom he knew I also wrote and who, according to David, was a mug for working for £2 a week.

I said in my letter that I had heard from Robert South, my American pal whom I had met in Baltimore in 1943. He was now demobbed from the Army and in his letter had said they he was sending me a Sheaffer pen and pencil set and a pen to my father. Although undependable, Robert was always generous and I was absolutely delighted with the pen when I eventually received it. It was the finest pen I ever possessed and found it a pleasure to write with. Several years later, something went wrong with it so that I took it to a shop in Hong Kong for repair where regrettably the nib was filed and destroyed. Robert had said also in his letter than he could send me any clothes I wanted. Apparently it was forbidden to send new

---

[20] This was in fact Leith Nautical College which I attended after the voyage and where I found my acquaintance's judgment to be absolutely 'spot on'.

clothes from the States, but one wash was sufficient to make them second-hand and there was no restriction on sending second-hand clothes. While I appreciated his offer, I never took it up.

George Brydges and Tony came into my cabin when I was typing that long letter and reprimanded me for typing it as it was considered 'infra dig' to type letters to relatives and friends. I commented on this in the letter and said that I had scrapped a couple of pages which I had written by hand the previous evening when the pen had been slipping from my fingers due to the heat. I also said that I doubted if either of my critics had written such a long letter and that as I wrote on a Yankee typewriter, it had only the $ and no £ sign. I had the radio on as I wrote and when during a Forces Favourites programme Annie Laurie was being sung, I said that it made me wish I were home. I added, however, that if Tico Tico were played, "they could take me down to Rio". In a later letter from Djibouti, I said that I now considered Tommy Handley, whose programme ITMA (It's That Man Again) had helped so much to keep up all our spirits during the early and grim dark days of the war, to be a 'pain in the neck'.

One day, when I went to the Post Office to enquire about stamps for collection, I was offered and bought a set of stamps of Tsad (Chad); then a district of French Equatorial Africa. I was offered nothing more, but on another occasion when I mentioned my interest in stamps to a Frenchman I met in a café, he took me to the Post Office and introduced me to the Postmaster. I was then able to purchase two sets of Djibouti stamps; one ordinary mail and one airmail. The ordinary set was of particular interest as prices had been superimposed on the stamps after Djibouti had been liberated. The Postmaster said that he had only four sets left and that they were in great demand by collectors. (The rate of exchange was 280.75 francs to £1.)

Another Frenchman I met was an operator at the radio station with which we communicated on entering and leaving the port. He was dressed in khaki shirt, shorts and sandals and wore a topi, but no stockings. I accepted his offer to come and see where he lived and, as he had given up a job on a French coast station to work in this God-forsaken place, I expected that he would live well. I couldn't have been more wrong. After tramping to the very edge of the town, when only the odd native braved the afternoon heat, I was shocked to find that he lived in a hut close to the dusty road which led into the desert. His room had a concrete floor and, devoid of decoration, it contained little more a cooker and the camp bed on which he slept. I felt there was something wrong here and when he asked me to meet him again on Saturday night I did not go as, anyway, it took a considerable effort to get to and from the ship.

Due to the difficulty of getting ashore, I did not go very often but occupied myself by exploring the bay in which we were anchored and which teemed with sharks and other fish. We had a number of small rafts on board and, clad in khaki shirt and shorts and without a hat, I paddled about the harbour on one of the rafts; sometimes landing at small rocky outcrops to gaze down at coral and sea anemones. It was a marine biologist's paradise and I began to gather specimens which were put into an aluminium tank, provided by Mr Turner, on the starboard side of the boat deck. Everyone came to see what I gathered: sea anemones, a very small crustacean with a head resembling that of a cow, a small octopus, a crab, a small fish and a piece of coral. The aquarium looked really good, but everything in it was found dead the following morning. It was a blow, but as we thought that the creatures were likely to have died through lack of oxygen, Mr Turner had the carpenter put an outlet tap in the tank and a hose to trickle seawater in from the top so that the water would be continually changing. I collected a few more specimens, but when we found them either dead or dying the next morning, the aquarium was abandoned.

Mr Gastall, the carpenter, became as keen as I was in investigating the creatures of the deep and fixed a wooden bench across one of the rafts on which two people could sit using the two paddles which he also made. It was already getting dark one evening when Peter Pratt, the middy, sat in front of us as we paddled towards the shore and as it was dark by the time we reached it, we shone torches into the water looking for specimens. After catching a crab in a net which I had made out of a piece of aerial wire and an old flag, we excitedly came across a small shark in the shallow water. We manoeuvred into position and Chippy, standing up, let fly with the harpoon which he had made. The result was hilarious. The shark, in the region of 2½ feet long, leapt out of the water and landed squarely in Peter's lap before it regained the water. And when we chided Peter for not keeping hold of it, he said that he had tried to although it didn't seem that way to us! But many of the sharks in the bay were enormous and at night the light at the top of the gangway, attracted them. When, late one evening, I saw one of the monsters swimming under the light, I dashed into Chippy's cabin to tell him. He was already in bed, but sprang up and grabbed a harpoon. But the creature had gone and I doubt if, anyway, his small harpoon would have had much effect on it. The bay was full of sharks. I sometimes saw shoals of smaller fish leap out of the water in an effort to escape from them and have often wondered what would have been the outcome had we speared one from our small raft. In Djibouti, swimming was never an option to escape from the heat and the coal dust.

We were the only vessel in port when we arrived, but a Swedish ship, a Frenchman, a Dutch tanker and two Greeks came in during our stay. The Swede didn't stay long and was as clean as the Greeks were dirty. And covered in coal dust, on the outside at least, we more closely resembled the Greeks. Using our winches and with natives down the holds shovelling the coal into buckets, our method of discharge was always primitive. In Port Said, the buckets were lowered over the side and tipped over by men in the barges while, in Massawa, the buckets had been emptied onto wagons on the quay. In Djibouti, a chute was erected opposite each of our 5 holds, the coal was tipped onto the chutes and shot, from a considerable height, into the barges alongside. This resulted in a great deal more noise and coal dust being produced when a bucket was emptied. Discharging coal in Djibouti was particularly dusty, hot and noisy.

There were always arguments/discussions on board ships, and after a political broadcast concerning housing in which Harry Pollitt, the leader of the British Communist Party, took part, there was a great argument in the saloon. The debate focused on the ownership of land and when Ernest stuck up for private ownership, Mr Turner said this was because he had been bequeathed a house and his wife had a couple of thousand (£s) in the bank! George wasn't present, but he generally lost his head in debates and particularly when religion was the topic under discussion. Although it seemed to me that he was no great advertisement for the cause, he always vociferously maintained that Christianity was the hope of the world. Mr Turner cracked the joke: "1st small boy:- Do you believe in Santa Claus? 2nd small boy:- Yes. 1st small boy:- It's just your father and, when I have time, I'm going to look into this Jesus business too!" Mr Turner had had the offer of a job as stevedore foreman with Mann, George & Co. in Lourenço Marques at a salary of £50 a month. He was keen to take the job, but, although the salary appeared good, he had heard that he'd need at least £60 a month to live comfortably and had written to the Company to see if they would increase the salary. During that discussion in the saloon, I learnt that his father and uncle had both been masters in the Merchant Navy.

I had just finished reading Nancy Mitford's 'In Pursuit of Love' which I considered a 'tripey' book and had commenced the 'Economic History of England' by Charlotte Waters which I had doubts about finishing. Ffoulkes had offered me a copy of 'The Ragged Trousered Philanthropists' by Robert Tressell, the pen name of Robert Noonan, and was just as surprised to learn that I had already read it as I was to have him offer it to me. The book is a little-known masterpiece describing the conditions under which a group of builders and decorators worked in the fictional town of Mugsborough (Hastings) in the early years of the 20th century. Noonan died of tuberculosis at the early age of 41 and was buried in a communal paupers' grave in Walton Cemetery, Liverpool, in 1911.

Our cargo was nearly out and it was anticipated that we would sail, for Lourenço Marques, during the evening of Wednesday, 20 November. Tony moved to the pilot's cabin on Tuesday morning and his cabin was thoroughly cleaned by the stewards to receive Mrs Dix and her daughter. In spite of Tony's generosity, the pilot's cabin got scant attention and this angered me so that I would liked to have been in Ffoulkes' position and done something about this. In my opinion, our stewards got away with murder and Tony's spotlessly clean cabin lay vacant overnight. Normally I did all the purser's work, but I had Tony type the list of overtime done by the crew in Djibouti and because he was no typist, this took him almost all day.

Our cargo of coal had required wooden dunnage to keep it in place. The Somalis were stealing the wood and this angered Mr Turner, as it would any Mate. When he found, on the Tuesday evening, that planks had been thrown into a barge into which coal was being discharged, he ordered the middies to get down into it and cast them into the sea. Perhaps he was right, but I thought this a mean act, unworthy of Mr Turner, as the wood was then lost to everybody. Ffoulkes was again ashore during the evening and as cargo working ended, the ship became quiet with most of us writing last letters home. As I wrote in my cabin, fellows continually came up with their letters for posting. And some of the letters from the younger seamen had the usual SWALK (Sealed With A Loving Kiss) printed on the back of the envelope.

It was a disgruntled Captain Ffoulkes who returned from the shore on the evening of 10 November and told me that he had spent the day with Mrs Dix and her daughter who had arrived by air and were to remain in an hotel until we ready to leave. Referring to the daughter, he said, "What she needs is a good spanking. She's spoilt. I'm afraid she'll be a bit of a nuisance to you next door." After signing on as Supernumerary Stewardess on Wednesday, 20 November, Mrs Dix and Denise boarded and took possession of Tony's cabin. But it was the following day before we sailed for Lourenço Marques, and, shortly after sailing, we communicated with the homeward bound *Samite* (BFPG) whose 2nd R/O had been landed into hospital in Colombo.

Postscript: Between 1883 and 1888, the French took possession of the territory which they named French Somaliland. In 1892, Djibouti, on the southern shore of the Gulf of Tadjoura and the main port, became the capital of the territory and, in 1917, a railway line was completed, connecting it with Addis Ababa in Ethiopia. Several years after our visit, the territory, still under French control, was renamed Afars and Issas, after the indigenous peoples, and, in 1977, became the Republic of Djibouti which retains strong links with France. But, when we were there the name Djibouti applied only to the town where the mean daily maximum temperatures range between 29°C and 41°C (July). The whole country is so hot and dry that less than 1% is arable and water for the town is obtained from an underground stream. In [21] 1946, the population of the town was less than 10,000, but today, owing to a massive influx of refugees from the Ethiopian-Somali conflict in the 1970s, it is now in the region of 150,000.

---

[21] The rate of exchange was 280.75 francs to £1.

20   BACK TO LOURENCO MARQUES

Throughout the passage to Lourenço Marques, we had a tropical cyclone on our tail; travelling in roughly the same direction at a speed which might allow it to catch us up. We copied all weather reports and on 27 November a cyclone warning stated that the spill was between Diego Suarez, at the northern tip of Madagascar, and Agalega, approximately 580 miles to the northeast. With only water ballast, we were particularly vulnerable; the ship rode high in the water and shook violently when the propeller rose clear of the water with every pitch. An anxious Ffoulkes was prepared to alter course if necessary and Mr Turner said that 'we might as well pack our hands in' if the cyclone caught us. But we saw nothing of it and would have been unaware of its presence, but for the existence of radio.

Tropical cyclones form in all the oceans of the world between latitudes 10°N and 15°N and 10°S and 15°S of the equator; near the equatorial region of low pressure. The winds, which can reach 150 mph or more, circle anti-clockwise round the centre in the northern hemisphere and clockwise in the southern hemisphere. The diameter of a cyclone may extend over hundreds of miles and while the whole mass moves slowly at first, its speed increases and can reach in excessive of 20 mph. The trade winds influence the direction of cyclones and although there are recognized cyclone tracks over the oceans, their paths and speeds are unpredictable. The Mozambique Channel and Madagascar lie directly in the track of the cyclones of the Southern Indian Ocean and it is in that area that cyclones, which have been travelling in a south-westerly direction, generally veer towards the southeast. Tropical cyclones are known as typhoons in the China Sea and the Pacific, and as hurricanes in the Caribbean and Atlantic.

Although our passenger lived next door to me for twelve days, she never spoke. Tony was not introduced to her and when she left the ship, his cabin was found to be in an absolute mess with powder and finger marks all over the place. We heard that her husband was paid the enormous salary of £1400 pa and Ernest claimed that she wore nine different dresses in one week. Her daughter, although only four, spoke Italian and a native language in addition to English. But, due to her mother's aloofness, I made no attempt to be friendly so that she remained in awe of me and I was spared the trouble anticipated by Ffoulkes.

Ffoulkes took it for granted that I should type all his letters to Our School and I didn't like this. He had a typewriter similar to mine, but I was the only one who could type and had he asked me to type the letters, I would willingly have done so. I had to do something about it and deliberately made an absolute mess of the exceedingly long letter which he gave me as we neared Lourenço Marques. He was soon at my door telling me that he couldn't send such a mess, but as it was only mess he had ever received, he got the message and I was henceforth, generally, relieved of the chore.

We dropped anchor in the harbour of Lourenço Marques at 8.30am on Monday, 2 December, 1946. The [22]Agent brought mail and the news that the coal which we had come to load was to be taken to Dar es Salaam and Tanga in Tanganyika. When he returned to the shore, our passengers went with him in the launch to complete their journey to South Africa by train. As there were two ships ahead of us waiting their turn at the coal tips, we were to remain at anchor for several days. I received in the order of a dozen letters dated between 22 October and 22 November and learned from their contents that earlier letters were missing.

I spent the afternoon of the day of our arrival and the following afternoon sunbathing on a camp bed on the bridge. But when Ffoulkes told me that he was going ashore on the Wednesday morning, I availed myself of the free ride in the launch and did some shopping. With Christmas on the horizon, I managed to buy a few poor Christmas cards plus two bottles of the Bastardo port wine which my father had raved about when I had brought some home the previous year. (Regarding the rate of exchange, the British Consulate stamp on the Articles read – 'BUYING Rate of Exchange for 3 day's SIGHT drafts on LONDON is 98$70 to the £ STERLING (for the conversion of seamen's Wages only).')

As we lay at some distance from the shore, the cost of a launch was expensive and I was not ashore again until we were taken alongside at 4.30pm on Saturday afternoon when loading immediately commenced. Coaling was fast in Lourenço Marques, but, as the coal was tipped into the holds from very large buckets, the noise created added to our discomfort. In order to get ashore, we had to run the gauntlet of coal-strewn decks, swinging buckets and coal dust. The dust even blew along the quay and,

---

[22] Thirty years later I learned from Ffoulkes that he had been offered a bribe by the Agent in Lourenço Marques. The tall scholarly-looking grey haired man, who I should have thought was beyond corruption, had opened a drawer in his office and, indicating the money lying there, said, "That's yours, Captain". But he had mistaken his man and, leaving the money untouched, Ffoulkes had replied, "My employer pays me."

when we got clear of the ship, we spat on our handkerchiefs and did our best to wipe it from our faces and hair. It was a far cry from the popular image of the prestigious Blue Funnel Line. And, as it was summer in the Southern Hemisphere, it was hot.

Ernest and I went to the lovely Vasco da Gama Gardens where we sat under the shade of a creeper woven into a bamboo structure. I nodded off to sleep, but was shortly awakened by a native attendant who said something in Portuguese which we could not understand. Ernest thought him a fool for wakening me, but perhaps the man considered it dangerous to sleep in the afternoon sun. We then walked over the hill, on which the European residential area stood, and came across a "Portugal Can Make It" exhibition which incorporated some sideshows. The exhibition was surrounded by a canvas enclosure, decorated by Portuguese flags and painted to resemble a medieval fortress. This was Ernest's first time ashore since we had last visited the port in October.

On the evening prior to sailing, Tony and I went to the Scala Cinema and bumped into Pieter Van Dijk who was on his own. He admonished me for not letting him know that we were in port and invited us to accompany him to the Penguin night club where a haggard middle aged woman made advances to him and mentioned bathing in the sea at midnight. When he asked if this were in the nude, she provocatively replied that he would have to come and see. And noticing my embarrassed silence, she remarked to Pieter, in Afrikaans, "Stille water, diepe grond".

We sailed for Dar es Salaam at 2am on 10 December, with a new Chief Engineer as Mr Quayle had been invalided home and replaced by Mr J Currie, from Largs.

21 DAR ES SALAAM

It was again a relief to get to sea and to have the decks hosed down to get rid of the coal dust although the relief was to be short-lived as it was only a short passage to Dar es Salaam. We received another cyclone warning that evening and, early on Thursday, a weather report stated that the cyclone was "centred approximately 11° South 43° East and may reach the African coast this morning". At 10.15 am our position was 22° 39′ South 36° 52′ East. Again we saw nothing of the cyclone and anchored in the outer harbour of Dar es Salaam at 4.08pm on Sunday 15 December. We were so fully laden that we could not be taken into the inner harbour until high tide the following morning and, even then, only after we had reduced our draft by discharging boiler water.

When the Sparks of the small BI (British India Steam Navigation Company) coaster *Sofala* heard us on the air during the passage from Lourenço Marques, he had called us up to let us know that they were also bound for Dar es Salaam and had mail for us. This welcome news was spread throughout the ship so that, after we had passed through the entrance and dropped anchor in the inner harbour at 9am on Monday, everyone eagerly awaited the arrival of the *Sofala* whose previous port was Tanga.

Discharging commenced and, once again, it was into barges towed to the shore. But, thankfully, the buckets were lowered into the barges and not tipped onto chutes as in Djibouti. Traders came alongside and sold us pineapples for 6d (2½p) and I have a clear recollection of standing eating the fruit and thinking what a good life this was: the *Samnesse* was a happy ship and I liked East Africa. This was a time, incidentally, when there was a flying boat service from the UK and we sometimes enjoyed the spectacle of these 'planes landing on or taking off from the water.

The *Sofala* docked at 1pm and a few hours later the Agent brought our mail on board. I received twelve letters, dated between 9 August and 30 November, some of which had been to Port Said and Genoa. In the evening, Ernest and I went ashore to see Nelson Eddy in 'Knickerbocker Glory'. At 3/- (15p), the uncushioned seats were expensive and the show lasted only 1¾ hours with a quarter of an hour interval. The shops, generally of the bazaar type, were almost exclusively owned by Indians. They were, however, well stocked and a made-to-measure shirt could be had for only 16/- (80p).

Due to the loss of a film by the excessive heat, I now took films ashore for developing, but continued to produce the prints. The ferrotype (a device to put a gloss on photographic prints) which my father had posted months earlier, had still not arrived and never did.

I reported on yet another negative reply from the Board of Trade in response to my request for clothing coupons although they had received the certificate of loss provided by the LMS. As I was gradually replenished my clothing abroad, it was the unfairness of their behaviour which rankled and, ironically, I still have a book of unused MN clothing coupons.

Ffoulkes interrupted my writing to ask me to fix the ribbon on his typewriter. I had told him that morning that the keys required cleaning and he had asked how to obtain access to them as he had tried to remove the front cover without success. But, when I removed the cover, he was taking no notice and talking about shirts which he had ordered so that, when he saw the keys exposed he exclaimed, "Now, how the devil...?". When I returned to my writing, Manuel de Fallas' Ritual Fire Dance was blaring from his loudspeaker as he laboriously typed a letter to 'Our School'.

As the entrance to the port is very narrow, it had been considered safe to swim in the harbour until a Norwegian sailor almost lost his life when attacked by a shark. Although apparently unprotected by nets, the safe place to swim was deemed to be the (Europeans only) swimming station near the harbour entrance. After a swim there, I returned to town by rickshaw and had my photograph taken as the 'pukka sahib' lolling back in the carriage.

We sailed at 4.37pm on Saturday, 21 December and arrived in Tanga at 6.35am the following day.

Postscript: The name Dar es Salaam is derived from the Arabic words dar salaam, meaning haven of peace, as Arab traders had established settlements in East Africa from the 1st century AD when their first incursions into the interior were for slaves and ivory. And the Arab legacy remains as Arabic is still spoken along the coast although English and Swahili are the official languages of Tanzania. In 1946, Dar es Salaam had a population of about 25,000 and was the capital of Tanganyika Territory, governed by Britain. Today its population is in the region of 3 million and in 1983 Dodoma replaced it as the capital of Tanzania.

22   CHRISTMAS IN TANGA

Tanga (The Sail) is situated in an elevated position above the bay. Similar to Dar es Salaam, it is the terminus of a railway line to the interior, and sisal was then its main export. We entered the bay through the broad channel and as again there were no docking facilities, anchored in the harbour. Barges were towed out to us and soon there was the familiar rattle of our winches as coal was discharged into barges.

It was my experience that when a ship lay at anchor, little or no consideration was shown to those on board who wanted to go ashore; no matter how long they had been at sea. Sometimes it was physically impossible to go while at other times the cost of a launch made it prohibitive. It was a pleasant surprise, therefore, when the Agent's launch came alongside the gangway at 3.30 pm on the day of our arrival for those of us who were free and wanted to go swimming. We grabbed our trunks and towels and the launch took us to a lovely beach (again Europeans only) which was deemed to be safe from sharks although, again, there was no net affording protection from them. We enjoyed the sport and the launch brought us back to the ship at 5pm.

One of the middies accompanied me the following morning when I made my first visit into town to collect cash for the crew at the Agent's office. We didn't hurry back, but had a wander around Tanga where, as in Dar es Salaam, the shops were owned mostly by Indians. In the afternoon, I washed yet another layer of coal dust from the walls of my cabin.

In the evening, I had difficulty in concentrating on writing a letter while listening to a programme of Christmas carols on the Overseas Service of the BBC; Christopher Stone was announcing the carols sung by a choir in Huddersfield City Hall. And, as we had been told at the beginning that we were joining Home Service listeners, I wondered if my folks were also listening.

Most of the crew were ashore on Christmas Eve so that it was a near-deserted ship which swung silently at anchor. I sat alone at the desk in my cabin, with the door open, when, most surprisingly, three young women, conducted by a seaman, emerged from the top of the stairs to the bridge deck and smiled as they passed on their way to see Captain Ffoulkes in his cabin on the starboard side. Not long afterwards, Ffoulkes appeared at my door and asked if I would like to go to a dance on Saturday night. When I said that I would, he told me to come round to his cabin to meet the girls who were nurses at the local hospital. Two were Scots and one Irish and they had come with invitations to the Captain and officers of his choosing to attend their dance on the evening of Saturday, 28 December. Mr Currie, the Chief Engineer, was already seated with a glass of whisky in his hand and we saw Christmas Day in by eating sandwiches, drinking tea and imbibing. In my case, this was a sherry and Ffoulkes was equally abstemious. I have no idea if the nurses had limited their invitation to only three, but at any rate only the three of us were to go to the dance and no doubt Mr Turner had been excluded because Ffoulkes would not entrust the ship into the care of anyone else.

There was no work on Christmas Day - a fact, I may say, which could never be taken for granted - and a boat came for those who wanted to go swimming. And as the Negroes rowed us to the bathing station, I felt it reminiscent of Edgar Wallace's 'Sanders of the River'! Our clothes were left in a hut guarded by a Negro and we had a great time plunging from the diving boards into the clear blue water in brilliant sunshine. There were two boards and I hit upon the idea of jumping from the higher board onto the lower one so that we sprang high into the air before entering the water. Tony, however, hurt his back which, he said, he might have broken. But it was a great way to spend a Christmas and a happy party which was taken back to the ship for Christmas Dinner. And the day was made even more enjoyable when we found letters awaiting our return.

Mr Sawle, the Chief Steward, had run out of Blue Funnel menu cards so that he typed the following on a piece of ordinary thin cardboard:

S.S. "Samnesse"   Xmas Day. 1946

<u>D I N N E R</u>
Creme of Tomato
Poached Fillets Cod. Anchovy.
Baked York Ham.Madere.
Creamed Spinach
Puree of Carrots & Turnips
Roast & Boiled Potatoes
Roast Turkey. Chipolata.
Fresh Salad
Pudding.Noel. Rum Sauce.
Christmas Cake.
Coffee

Capt.A.J.Ffoulkes.

I am able to reproduce the menu because I still have that piece of cardboard which all the officers signed.

A group of us went ashore in the evening, but, as there were no places of entertainment open, we just wandered around. When we came to the Tanga Hotel, we found a dance in progress, but it was soon made clear to us that outsiders were not admitted as Dumbill, our assistant steward, was in the middle of a diatribe directed at the few men who had come out onto the veranda for a smoke. And with a drink inside him, Dumbill was most eloquent. "I remember you lot in Singapore," he was saying. "You were not so stuck-up then when you were looking to us to get you out." I deduced that he had been on a ship in Singapore when it was falling to the Japanese in 1942 and was, in my opinion, rightly angry that the same breed of British colonials, were showing their gratitude by excluding him and his shipmates, who stood quietly beside him, from their Christmas dance. As Rudyard Kipling so aptly put it when referring to the British soldier: ...."For it's Tommy this, an' Tommy that, an' Chuck him out, the brute! But it's Saviour of 'is country when the guns begin to shoot..."

The hospital dance required formal dress. I had no white jacket, but Alan Curry lent me his and I was well turned out. Ffoulkes was similarly clad, but to his ill-concealed annoyance, Mr Currie showed up in a lounge suit and wearing a dark tartan shirt.

The dance was held in the Palm Court Hotel; a name familiar to us as every Sunday evening the Palm Court Orchestra, conducted by Albert Sandler, broadcast from a similarly named hotel in London. But while the Palm Court in Tanga had palm trees round it, it had no orchestra so that we danced to music provided by a radiogram. Apparently there was only one band in Tanga; an Indian one which played only at Indian dances. There was a great turnout of British colonials, many of whom spent almost their entire lives abroad, and everyone I met was polite and friendly. A man and his wife spoke of life in Britain. It was, they said, so very different from the country they had known before the war, that, even apart from the climate, they didn't want to live there any more. The Provincial Governor, a tall austere man, was present and, running around in his attendance, was a small young man from Edinburgh whose attractive wife, also from Edinburgh, was there too.

I considered the proceedings to be pretty dull until the grub came along and a little Glasgow nurse made sure that I got enough to eat. Then the radiogram broke down and someone, knowing my profession, said to me,

"Come on, you should know something about it" to which I replied, "Yes, I know I should know something about it." A small gramophone, with a 'pick-up' connection to the speaker in a wireless set, was then brought out and I was spared any embarrassment. By about half-an-hour after midnight, Ffoulkes and I had had enough, but Mr Currie declined to leave with us as he was enjoying the free whisky.

We were about to climb into the Agent's car which was to convey us to the landing stage, when a fellow came along in a lorry and insisted that we come to the Club for a 'snorter'. The Club was near the hotel and we went there with this fellow and two young men from the Agent's office. One of the young men and I had a game of snooker which I won on the black just before Ffoulkes was able to spoil the game by wanting a shot! In attendance in the snooker room was a tall black man, dressed in galabiah and turban, who, even at 2 o'clock in the morning, had the job of picking the balls out of the pockets. It was 3am before I got into my bunk after a very educational experience although it was disconcerting to a Blue Funnel man to be asked if he were off the coal ship!

We now knew our next port-of-call. It was Durban again and while the married men were always looking to going home, most of us were unattached and didn't give a hoot. But there was much speculation as to why it was Durban and not Lourenço Marques and some deduced from this that we were now off the coal run. But, in a letter home, on which I made a deliberate coal-dust thumb print, I said I wouldn't be surprised if we went under the coal tips at the Bluff. We sailed from Tanga on the afternoon of Monday, 30 December and estimated that we would be in Durban by about 6 January, 1947.

Postscript: Tanganyika Territory, formerly German East Africa, was mandated to Britain by the League of Nations after the defeat of Germany in the Great War of 1914-18. In July, 1914, the German cruiser *Konigsberg* steamed out of Dar es Salaam and, in September, sank the British light cruiser *Pegasus* off Zanzibar. In August, 1914, the British cruiser *Astraea* bombarded Dar es Salaam, but her gunnery officer got some ribbing when it was later discovered that the brewery had been destroyed!

In November, 1914, an Indian Army force landed at Tanga and met with disaster. The British Battalion of the Bangalore Brigade succeeded in reaching the main hotel, which is likely to have been the Tanga Hotel where Dumbill made his speech, and hauled down the German flag. But, receiving little support from the main body of inexperienced Indian troops and being submitted to what is now euphemistically known as friendly fire, from the supporting guns of HMS *Fox*, they were forced to withdraw. In addition to all this, they were stung unmercifully by African bees which are much more virulent than our own. The Germans suffered equally from their ministrations, but such was Colonel von Lettow's reputation that the British officers actually believed them to be part of his strategy.

On the conclusion of the Second World War, Tanganyika became a United Nations Trust Territory, still administered by Britain. In 1961, and renamed Tanzania, it became an independent country and, a year later, declared itself a republic within the British Commonwealth. In 1964, the already independent island of Zanzibar, united with Tanzania to form the United Republic of Tanzania.

23   THIRD VISIT TO DURBAN

The passage to Durban was fairly good, but again in water ballast, the ship rolled and pitched a great deal. Every weather report contained information on tropical cyclones and, as we neared the Mozambique Channel, there was one to the northeast and another over southwest Madagascar. But without ever altering course, it was again our good fortune to escape their attention with only a heavy swell indicating the distant presence of a storm. Sometimes we were enveloped in heavy showers of rain and one night we experienced a violent thunderstorm. But the "Samnesse" made good speed and one day we bowled along at a phenomenal 15 knots although our maximum speed was only 12½. In our book, this made us a veritable ocean greyhound and was due to the aid of the Agulhas Current which flows north to south along the East African coast. But our elation dissipated rapidly when the steering gear broke down during the evening of Friday, 3 January and speed was reduced to 4 knots. The sea had become moderately rough and the ship was merely kept under weigh until connection was made to the emergency steering wheel on the poop.

Purser's work kept me busy during the passage and Ffoulkes added to it by having me type some his letters to Barnstaple Girls' Grammar School which I had begun to refer to as His and not Our School. But I now had no defence as he had taken to *asking* me to type his letters. Writing to the School had become his hobby and, quite frankly, I and others on board, were browned off with it as he was altogether too keen. When I had been ashore with him in Dar es Salaam, he had wormed his way into three of my snaps and, in Tanga, had paid for the development of films. Now, when I was doing the printing, he wanted so many copies that he was getting the best of the bargain. But, to be fair to Captain Ffoulkes, he now typed most of his long and interesting letters himself and spent long hours at the task. I, equally, spent long hours typing some of his letters and producing the photographic prints which he sent and, as I re-did prints to improve upon the result, the wastage of printing paper was considerable. I frequently added to this wastage when I left prints stuck too long on the mirror of my toilet cabinet mirror as this was how I produced a gloss on them. It was difficult to judge the optimum time and, when I overshot it, they had to be scraped off.

I had fallen behind with my dhobi and would dearly liked to have been spared the effort of doing it by having it done by a laundry in Durban. But, the Indians who owned the, not yet steam, laundries made a poor but costly job and were unreliable. On our previous visit Ernest had lost a pair of flannel trousers which he had sent for cleaning and had got back a scruffy pair of white shorts in place of the good ones he had sent. All on board, including Captain Ffoulkes, did their own washing.

The New Year of 1947, was quietly ushered in on our way to Durban. The English, Welsh and Irish, aware of its importance to the four Scots on board, made us pay for drinks. But they were a pretty abstemious lot and, at duty free prices, my Steward's Account didn't suffer much. Incidentally, we usually saw the Comoros in the distance when negotiating the Mozambique Channel and it was claimed by Mr Turner that the most beautiful women in the world lived on the islands although I have no idea if he spoke from experience! About 300 miles from the port, we contacted Durbanradio so that our impending arrival was reported in the Daily News and all girlfriends alerted!

It was summer holiday time in South Africa and, when the pilot boarded to take us in, we could see hordes of sun-bathers on the beach. As we passed slowly between the Bluff and the town, people out for their Sunday stroll stopped to gaze at the ship coming in and girls waved to us. And, at 2.36pm, on Sunday, 5 January, we tied up, once again, at the coal tips of the Bluff, beside the Argentinean *Parana*. An enterprising photographer had taken a picture of the *Samnesse* as she entered and when my son recently looked at the framed copy in my study, his only comment was "She looks dirty." But, she was a happy ship and, to any sailor, this is the highest accolade which can be paid to any ship. Ships with fine lines, and there are few of them today, can be little more than sweatboxes and as to whether a ship is happy or not depends, almost entirely, on the master.

Despite the disappointment of learning that we were still on the coal run and about to load our fourth cargo of the stuff, we were happy to be back in Durban after an absence of approximately 3 months. Our berth, however, not a convenient one for access to the town. We were near the oiling station. It was a 20-minute walk along the quay, past other ships loading coal, to the Bluff Ferry which conveyed us to the Point and the whole journey took at least 45 minutes. The Ferry, however, ran till midnight, with the 15 minute service reduced to a half-hourly one after 7pm, and the ship was almost deserted that first night in port.

I always liked being on board when the ship was quiet and particularly when she swung at anchor in the harbours of East Africa. On such occasions, when I played records on my portable wind-up gramophone, I knew that others too were enjoying the music. And Handel's Largo has never been played in a better setting to a more appreciative audience. I did not, however, play only classical music as I equally liked the dance band recordings of the time.

There was one such evening when C. Griffin, AB appeared at the door of my cabin when I was sitting at my desk beside my ever-open door. He was the man who had pressed me for the Advance Note at the beginning of the voyage and, at 49 years of age, was by far the oldest seaman on board. A small dapper man with thinning white hair and a trim moustache, he spoke with an upper class English accent. He had been drinking and it was the influence of drink which encouraged him to climb the two flights of stairs to the bridge deck to see me. Leaning against the jamb of the door, he asked if I had my School Certificate. This was an English qualification which, as a Scot, I had only heard of although I knew it to be superior to the one I had on leaving school at the age of 14. When I replied that I did not, he said, "Well, I have" and went on to tell me that he had been an Inspector in the South African Police. But, even in his cups, there was no suggestion that he regretted his downfall due to drink and it appeared to me that he was happy as an AB. But, having learned something of his background, I was shocked to hear him using the most obscene language when working on deck among his peers.

I again enjoyed myself in Durban and, although it took only two days to load us, it was a week before loading commenced. And it was only when I went down for breakfast one morning that I learned that there had been a commotion during the night as a Negro, apparently intent on robbery, had been discovered on board. It appeared that everyone else had been involved in the disturbance which I slept through.

Once again I went to the pictures and to dances at the Mission and the MN Officers' Memorial Club. Admission to the latter was strictly controlled and I still have the small linen-type cards which gave me honorary membership in 1946 and 1947. But the activities of the Mission were available to all ranks and I have the greatest admiration for the padre and his staff. Their lives were devoted to doing their best for merchant seamen and the young padre and his wife boarded every ship which entered the port to welcome her in. I sent off another food parcel from the Mission, but the facility of posting free mail there was no longer available as the Fleet Mail Office had closed.

On the morning of 14 January, Ffoulkes and I went to the Shipping Office to pay off J. Barnard, the South African fireman who had joined us in Lourenço Marques in October, and to witness the signing on of his replacement - 20-year-old Irishman W.J. Blakeney; a deserter from the *Fort Gaspereau*. This business concluded, we went shopping together and, when I bought a somewhat colourful sports jacket at Payne Bros and Ffoulkes expressed disapproval, the shop assistant respectfully pointed out the difference in our ages. The jacket cost £7-2/- (roughly the equivalent of a week's wage), while flannel trousers and black shoes, which I also bought in Durban, cost £3-10/- and £1.7.6d respectively.

In the afternoon I played football for the *Samnesse* against another ship. It was tiring work playing in the heat of the afternoon with the temperature touching 28°C and the backs of my legs subsequently ached from the unaccustomed exercise. We were beaten by 4 to 1, but I emerged a hero by scoring our solitary goal.

At 6.45 am on Thursday, 16 January, 1947 we sailed for Port Said, via Aden. And, most regretfully, I never again visited the beautiful City of Durban or, for that matter, any other port in East Africa.

24   PORT SAID VIA ADEN (AGAIN)

In those days, when we spent much longer in port than sailors have done since the advent of the container ship, we almost always liked being at sea again. There was something satisfying about leaving the noise and bustle of the shore, not to mention coal dust, and resuming the quiet routine of life in our own little world.

Mr Turner wanted to send a message to Mann, George & Co. in Lourenço Marques and suggested to me that, rather than pay for its transmission through the local radio station, I could ask the R/O of a ship heading for the port to accept and deliver it. I did this and the obliging R/O delivered the message personally. Although this was the first such irregular action in my sea-going career, it was not the last.

Smiling broadly, Captain Ffoulkes told me to have a look at the notice board on the boat deck. On the board was a drawing cut out of the January 23 1946 issue of the magazine "Punch". It depicted a bespectacled radio officer, wearing earphones, with a mug of tea in his hand, on watch in a wireless room. The room was in chaos with clothes strung on lines attached to the deck head, a bucket and a teapot in evidence, and piles of papers on the desk. A master was attempting to enter the room and the caption was "Are you busy just now Mr. Wilkinson?" Ffoulkes' comment was, "He (the artist) couldn't have done it better if he'd known you." I subsequently learned that Mr Turner had pinned the cartoon to the board and Norman Mansbridge, the artist, did know of my ilk, as he had served as an R/O during the war.

The weather became pleasantly cooler as we headed north and, within a week of reaching Aden, it was cool enough at night to have a sheet over me in bed. As, apart from my radio watch, I could work when I liked, I preferred to spend afternoons sunbathing and work at my desk in the evenings. There was, of course, always the accursed dhobi to do and I kept it down by doing a little every day. Washing clothes in a small washbasin and ironing them on a small desk was a major chore so that I regard the washing machine as one of mankind's greatest inventions. During the passage, my reading consisted mainly of the short stories in issues of the monthly magazine 'Argosy' which, together with the 'Wide World Magazine', I bought regularly.

As ships going to and coming from the East, the Persian Gulf, East Africa and Australia converged on the Gulf of Aden, the ether became busier as we neared Aden. This time we were in contact with the *Ascanius* (GPZC) whose last port-of-call had been Colombo and was homeward bound via Aden. Built in 1910, she had come through both World Wars as a troopship. And, still trooping, she kept continuous radio watch and had four R/Os on board.

We anchored off Steamer Point, at about 8.30am on Wednesday 29 January, and, while we had been keeping watch or sleeping comfortably in our bunks during the night, a tragedy was being enacted on one of our sister ships in the Atlantic. Homeward bound from Australia, the *Samwater* was approximately 35 miles west of Cape Finisterre when fire broke out in her engine room. The fire spread so rapidly that the engineers were unable to reach the controls to shut down the engines, and it was this factor which led to the loss of life when she had to be abandoned in a moderately rough sea. The lifeboats were launched when she was still under weigh and when one capsized, all of its occupants (seventeen crew and two passengers) were thrown into the sea and lost their lives. As the ship's power supply had been cut off due to the fire, and the emergency batteries failed to function, a distress message could not be sent. The Swedish ship *P.L. Pahlsson*, which was not equipped with radio, but had been spoken to earlier by Aldis lamp, picked up the twenty-six from the other two lifeboats and landed them in Lisbon the following day.

The Agent brought out a small amount of mail and I went ashore on business and to post parcels for Ffoulkes and Mr Turner. In the Post Office, a deck apprentice enquired as to the ship I was from and, when I told him, he said he was from the Brocklebank ship. He was a friendly chap, but the manner in which he spoke led me to ask, somewhat facetiously, if his name were Brocklebank. And to my surprise, he replied that it was and that he was at sea to learn the practicalities of the business before participating in management. Lawrence Holt's son, Julian, underwent the same rigorous training and these sons of owners enjoyed no privileged treatment as apprentices.

Aden remained a British Colony until 1967 when it became part of the People's Republic of Southern Yemen. And the years preceding the end of British rule were bloody indeed.

With our bunkers replenished, we sailed at about 4.30pm the same day and, after an uneventful passage through the Red Sea, anchored in Suez Bay at 7pm on Monday, 3 February with the lights of Suez and Port Tewfik twinkling in the near distance.

Always looking for mail, we awaited the arrival of the Agent and eager eyes spotted the mailbag on the floor of his launch as it approached the gangway. And, when the middies lugged the bag up to my room, the first item to emerge was a parcel, bearing franked UK stamps, addressed to me. I thought vaguely that I recognized the writing, but the sender had omitted to put his or her name on the back and I could not guess whom it was from. As no-one ever received parcels, everyone present was interested to see what it contained and all eyes were on me as I removed the brown paper wrapping. And a howl of laughter went up when the contents turned out to be two packets of Crunchies (wheat flakes) accompanied by a note saying, "Happy crunchin', Starvation". Because George Brydges also liked his food, I immediately thought that he had played the joke, but it was Mr Turner who had accepted the job in Lourenço Marques and was leaving the ship at Port Said. Captain Ffoulkes was in on the joke and enjoyed it even more the following morning when he found Tony and me tucking into huge platefuls of crunchies accompanied by tinned milk and lots of sugar. And George complained about not being invited to the feast! Almost all the mail we received was 4 months old.

Shortly after the departure of the Agent, a Canal pilot boarded and, with the required large searchlight at our bow to light our way, we entered the Canal immediately ahead of the *Stentor* (GMTC). We had communicated with her when she was well behind us in the Red Sea, but, with her superior speed, she had caught up with us. At that time, when the Canal was jointly owned by Britain and France, the pilots were either British or French and their highly paid, prestigious, job was surpassed only by that of the Hooghli River pilots who took ships to and from Budge Budge and Calcutta.

It was anticipated that we would be in Port Said early the following morning, but this notion was dispelled by a message from Ismailia Radio (call sign SUQ) soon after we entered the Canal. In fog, the *Star of Egypt* had hit the bank and was blocking the Canal. The result of this was that we spent the greater part of Tuesday in the Bitter Lakes waiting for the passage to be cleared and then for other south-bound vessels to come through. It was 4pm before we again got under way to complete the remaining 57 miles to Port Said. With the daytime temperature now lower, we had changed into blues that morning and, after so long in shorts, I felt it strange to have my knees covered. We tied up stern-to the breakwater on the eastern side of Port Said harbour at 0040 hours on Wednesday, 5 February and began discharging our coal, into barges, later in the day.

When I saw the 1921 *Glaucus* (GDXZ) in port, I had an Arab row me across to her in order to obtain some radio department stock sheets. Her No.1 was ashore so that I had to deal with his No.2 who, most surprising, turned out to be Neville Caro who still had only his Special Ticket. I was not wearing epaulettes, and he asked if I were No.1 'over there'. I, of course, replied that I was although I knew that he already knew the answer as we had communicated with him when he had been on *Antilocus* the previous August. He then went on to excuse his lack of certification by saying that he had no intention of remaining at sea, whereupon I replied that neither had I. And this was the truth as I never ever intended to spend my life at sea. As the Special Certificate remained valid on merchant ships only until the end of 1946, it now appears to me that, in February, 1947, Caro was no longer qualified to be a radio officer in the Merchant Navy.

Being paid less than Tony was a thorn in my flesh. When I had complained to Ffoulkes soon after we sailed from Tilbury and, expecting that we would be away for only about three months, he had said he would see about it when we returned home. But, when the details of Holt's new pay scales, operative from 1 January, arrived in Port Said, Tony's salary was increased to £24 a month and mine to only £23. I now asked Ffoulkes to write to Holts and he said to write a letter to him about the matter and he would forward it together with a letter expressing his opinion.

As I felt that I was being unfairly treated, I wrote a somewhat aggressive letter to Ffoulkes, but, on his advice, reworded it to *suggest* rather than *demand*. The rewrite, which I handed to him on Tuesday, 11 February, met with his approval but when he added, "Of course, they may do nothing about it", I replied, "If they don't, I'll ask to sail as 2nd Sparks again next trip". The word 'again' now amuses me as I had been 2nd Sparks for only five weeks!

Ffoulkes called me through to his cabin the next morning and showed me his letter which was to accompany mine. In it he said, "....I should like to say that although he has the least sea service, he is definitely the better officer of the two. This is not to the detriment of Mr Raven." I was, of course, flattered by his appraisal of me, but was taken aback by his approach; it had never been occurred to me to compare myself with Tony, but only to receive monetary recognition for the position of responsibility.

On 31st March and 1st April, 1947, what were described as 'the most far-reaching series of agreements ever negotiated by the National Maritime Board on behalf of shipmasters, officers and ratings and shipowners' came into effect. The £10 a month (£5 for those under 18) War Risk Money was incorporated into wages and wages were improved. But, for the majority of merchant seamen, the improved conditions of service were of greater importance. When the Merchant Navy Reserve Pool, a wartime arrangement financed by the taxpayer, ended on 31st March, an Established Service Scheme, offering two-year contracts, came into operation and this gave seamen continuity and security in employment. And leave, or payment in lieu, was given for Sundays spent at sea. It was a far cry from the conditions which obtained prior to May, 1942 when the War Bonus was only £5 a month (£2-10/- for those under 18) and both wages and Bonus ceased, on the grounds that no work was done after a ship was sunk.

We received a great deal of mail in Port Said, but, regarding mail sent from the ship, Ernest complained to Ffoulkes that it was lying too long in my care before being given to the Agent. His complaint was justified as, although Ffoulkes went ashore every morning to the Agent's office, he refused to take our letters on the grounds that the Agent should not be troubled every day. Even when Tony had offered to take it to Stapledon's office when he was going ashore, Ffoulkes had forbidden him to do so. Defending himself, Ffoulkes said that he always took the letters in time to catch the mail 'planes although I doubted if he knew their schedule! And as mail still went free of charge, the Agent had only to deliver it to the Fleet Mail Office.

On 13 February I saw to the paying-off of George Brydges and fireman J. Shaw who were both landed into hospital. George had suffered from an ingrowing toenail for several months and Mr Shaw, who had joined us in Port Said the previous August, had acute dermatitis in his face and legs. K.S. Crawford was signed on to replace George, and George was to replace him as 3rd Mate of the *Glaucus* when he left hospital. Mr Turner was now living in an hotel waiting to go to Cairo to board a 'plane for Lourenço Marques and T.J. Arch had come out from Liverpool to replace him. Mr Arch had an intense interest in football and knew all the teams in the leagues, who played for them and why.

I listened to Geraldo and swiped at cockroaches as I wrote home and referred to the revocation, by the Ministry of Labour and National Service, of the Essential Work (Merchant Navy) Orders of 1942. The Orders were revoked on 31 December, 1946 and this resulted in such an exodus from the MN that there was talk of the Orders being reintroduced. But they never were.

With all our coal discharged, we weighed anchor at 5.56 pm on Friday, 14 February, 1947 and, with a pilot to convey us out of the harbour, sailed slowly past the statue of de Lesseps into the Mediterranean. We were bound for Venice, 1300 miles away, and, as this was about a five-day run for us, we expected to be there by Wednesday the 19th.

25   ENROUTE TO VENICE

Peter Pratt had bought a monkey in East Africa. It always sat on the potato locker on the port side of the boat deck and, as well as feeding it, we frequently teased the animal so that it sprang at us until restrained by the rope by which it was tethered. But the weather had become too cold for the monkey and, as the potato locker was beside an engine room skylight, it had attempted to enter to obtain warmth. It had, however, missed its footing and it was like a death in the family the morning we found it strangled and hanging into the engine room.

All Europe was in the grip of one of the severest winters of the century. There had been a distinct chill in the air in Port Said and it became increasingly colder as we headed north. For the first three days of the passage, the weather was not too bad but, when we entered the Adriatic, a full gale was blowing with rough seas and visibility so poor that the navigators became uncertain of our position. Again light-ship, we were being tossed all over the place and it was a dirty night indeed when Ffoulkes asked me to provide D/F bearings. But this presented the problem of where to find the shore-based radio beacons on which to obtain a 'fix' as the book which I had listing the beacons was useless because pre-war beacons had not yet been restored.

To obtain a ship's position by direction finder, it is necessary to obtain bearings on two radio stations transmitting from known positions some distance apart. A bearing on one station establishes only the ship's direction from that station, but does not give distance. A bearing on another station is necessary as it is only, after taking into account the estimated distance travelled by the ship in the time interval between the bearings, where the bearings lines cross is the ship's position. But, as the distance covered by the ship in the interval has to allow for such factors as wind speed, current and tide, it is very much an estimate and particularly so in bad weather.

After spending time listening to coast stations (not radio beacons) working on 500 kcs, I obtained two bearings, on the direction finder in the chart room, with the navigating officer noting the precise time when each was taken. And, as the coast stations were working only intermittently, I had to be quick. When the 'fix' (where the bearings crossed) was obtained and it placed us about twenty miles from the position worked out by the mates'

[23]'dead reckoning', Ffoulkes said that my bearings were rubbish. But, when visibility had improved by the morning, he told me that I had been right. During later years, I learnt that this was the norm; D/F bearings were almost always pronounced as 'rubbish' with an apology ensuing.

Exact time is necessary to calculate longitude so that it was important for the navigating officers to know of any difference between the time shown on the ship's chronometer and Greenwich Mean Time (now often referred to and particularly by foreigners, as Universal Time Constant). It was the 2nd Mate's job to record the difference and he did this with the assistance of the radio department. At specified times, Rugbyradio (GBR) broadcast the time signal on the long-wave frequency of 16 kcs and, at Ernest's request, we would tune into Rugby. An electric buzzer connected the wireless room with the chart room and one of us would stand with a finger on the buzzer, listening to the pips which preceded the dash indicating the hour. When we pressed the buzzer, exactly on the dash, Ernest, in the chart room with his eyes on the chronometer, recorded the difference. I should mention that I was then ignorant of the fact that I could have requested the coast stations to send continuous signals in order to obtain bearings although a charge would have been made for this service.

Due to modern technology, the job of the radio officer has become obsolete and, with the introduction of the Global Positioning Service (GPS), using satellites, navigation is simple. With GPS, a ship's position can be ascertained to within fifty to a hundred metres and with P-Code Differential GPS accuracy can be within one metre. This makes it possible for people, sitting in front of control panels ashore, to guide unmanned ships across the oceans; a frightening scenario and anathema to all those interested in the sea.

It had become increasing cold and, during the two or three nights before we reached Venice, I shivered in my bunk as there was no heat in the radiators. It was only when Venice, under a light cover of snow, was sighted, that the heating was put on and, because we had been delayed by the weather, it was Thursday, 20 February before a pilot took us up the Canale Della Giudecca to the Stazione Marittima. As we entered the Canale, we passed close to the town centre and could see the people

---

[23] This was the term used to explain how navigators estimated a ship's position when they were unable to see either the sun or stars and use their sextants. And, as this condition might last for days on end, all they could do was work out a rough estimate after taking into account the factors described above.

wrapped up against the cold. We tied up at 12.05pm at a berth on the eastern mole; within sight of the 2½-mile causeway which connects Venice, by road and rail, to the mainland. And, most importantly, the representative of Bassani S.A., our Agents, brought mail.

26   VENICE

The journey to the St. Mark's Square took over an hour. It was a good 20-minute walk to the Piazzale Roma and a further 35 to 40 minutes, through the Grand Canal, by waterbus. The waterbuses, owned by Azienda Comunale di Navigazione Interna Lagunare, were fairly large steamboats which provided shelter from the elements and the fare was 12 lire (2½d/1p). It was a most enjoyable journey, passing under the Rialto Bridge and often enhanced by a man playing a mandolin. And, of course, there were the gondolas which were then not decorated for tourists, but confined to the mundane task of conveying people across the canals.

It was the first time Venice had seen snow in six years. There was no coal to heat the houses and, although some women wore fur coats and woollen stockings, the majority of the people were not as well dressed as those in Britain. But, by the day following our arrival, the snow had almost disappeared and it was a pleasure to walk in the, uniquely, traffic-free town. The motor road from the mainland ends at the Piassale Roma where there was a garage which could accommodate over 1000 cars and had places reserved for buses, motorbikes and bicycles. There were beggars in the streets and we noticed this because they had disappeared from the streets in Britain during the wartime years of full employment. And they were not seen again until the 1980s.

On our previous visits to Italy, the rate of exchange had been L.900 to the £1 sterling, but, while the Agent had informed me that a higher rate now applied, I didn't know exactly what it was until the Articles came back from the British Consulate. On the Articles, the Vice-Consul, had written by hand "Pending confirmation of new exchange rate, the rate for conversion of seamen's wages would appear to be Lire 1200 = £1". This was the only time that I saw the words, 'would appear to be', used. Paper money was issued by the wartime Allies and contained notes for as little as L.10. Heading the front of the notes it said 'Allied Military Currency' and, on the reverse side the same message was surrounded by the words 'Freedom of Speech', 'Freedom of Religion', 'Freedom from Want' and 'Freedom from Fear'. Although the war had ended eighteen months previously, our mail went free and was franked 'Maritime Mail' or 'Field Post Office'.

Ken Crawford, Tony and I went to the Teatro La Fenice (Opera House) to see "Pelléas et Mélisande" by Debussy. Three rows in the Theatre were reserved for Allied Forces; the front row, the back row and one in the middle of the stalls. I had booked seats in the front row and, as they cost only L.550 (9/- or 45p), I assume that this was a special price for the Forces. We were each given a free copy of the programme, in English, prepared by the military 'Education 86 Area' and typed on two quarto sheets stapled together, but we bought copies of the Theatre's programme as souvenirs. I must say that we didn't like either the miserable story of the opera or the music, but it was an uplifting experience to enjoy the atmosphere and beautiful decoration of the auditorium.

The Fenice was totally destroyed by fire on the night of 29 January, 1996 and was appropriately named as the name means Phoenix and it had been razed to the ground by fire on two previously occasions. This time, all the signs pointed to arson.

Ron Blundell, Ken Crawford and I had a guided tour of the Doges' Palace and gazed in wonder at the beautiful paintings and decorated ceilings. Among the former is Tintoretto's Paradise, the largest oil painting in the world.

We crossed the Bridge of Sighs to visit the Pozzi prisons and had the door closed behind us in one of the eighteen stone cells. Prisoners of the Republic had lived in total darkness, so that they lost their sight, and the only furniture was the wood covered bench which served as a bed.

On the evening of the same day, Ffoulkes came to my cabin with a plan of Venice and spread it out on my desk. "I've been studying this", he said, "and can see that we can walk into town with only a short crossing over the Grand Canal." The next day, when we crossed the Canal by gondola, he reprimanded me for giving more than the fare. "You must understand", he said, "that people have to use this service all the time and what you did is likely to encourage gondoliers to increase their charges." We walked to St. Mark's Square and were surprised to find that it was quicker to walk into town than to go by waterbus. But we returned by the waterbus after visiting the Cathedral.

Although the shops were, incomprehensibly, better stocked than those in Britain, prices were high and the black market was still flourishing. Vendors sold American and British cigarettes in the streets and we could still make a profit by selling our duty free ration. In spite of our earlier experience, Tony had accepted a counterfeit note and I was with him when he entered a small shop to make an inconsequential purchase to get rid of it. After holding the note up to the light, the young shopkeeper said that he couldn't accept it, but was so courteous and polite that we were both glad that he had spotted it. Apropos the black market, Ffoulkes told me that a much better rate of exchange could be had by selling British currency. When I replied that this was illegal and part of the black market he abhorred, he didn't know what to say!

Several of us bought musical instruments and there were now several mouth organs, three guitars, a mandolin and a piano accordion on board. When the football results were pinned to the notice board that evening, both Dundee and Dundee United had lost!

Field Marshal Albert Kesselring, who had commanded the German forces in Italy, was being tried as a war criminal, by a military court in Venice. He was brought to the mole by motor launch and it became part of our daily routine to watch him arrive and climb the stone steps to the quay, only yards from the ship. He had been branded a war criminal because he had ordered the Ardeatine cave massacre of 335 Italian hostages, in March 1944, in reprisal for an attack by partisans on German troops. The court, subsequently, found him guilty and sentenced him to death. But, with the incomprehensible leniency shown to so many of his murderous ilk, his sentence was commuted to life imprisonment and he was pardoned and freed in 1952. He then lived comfortably on a pension far in excess of the amount which the majority of us who had fought against the Nazis could earn working, and died, at the age of 75, in 1960.

We listened regularly to 'Shipmates Ashore' and hoped that the ships' newspaper section would provide information on the new wages and conditions. But it reported only on such matters as how many troops the Queen Elizabeth had carried, the ships being built for companies and recently there had been a synoptic history of Blue Funnel.

Captain Ffoulkes received a letter from Holts regarding my salary. Dated 21 February, 1947, it said Quote "....Please inform him that, in accordance with our new scale, he will be eligible for a [24]bonus for purser's work of

---

[24] Holts raised the purser's bonus in order to retain 1st R/Os as Pursers as they were leaving the Company because of the inadequate payment when they had the additional burden of cargo work. And, after two years as purser, the bonus was £6. The bonus was never shown on the Articles and, as the title of purser doesn't appear beside that of 1st R/O, anyone looking at copies of Articles today will wonder why Class II ships carried two R/Os.

£4.0.0. per month which brings his total earnings well above Mr. Raven's, and we will discuss the matter with him when he is next in this Office." When I presented myself at the Office, at the end of the voyage, my basic pay was adjusted to equal that of Tony's, throughout the voyage. I was pleased that my protestations bore fruit as Holts were under no legal obligation to make the additional payment.

We had come to Venice to load ammunition, guns and vehicles for the British Army and, by late Saturday, loading was completed. With six soldiers and a lieutenant on board, we sailed for Tripoli, in Libya, at 10.43 am on Sunday, 2 March, 1947.

Postscript: Venice is situated on an archipelago of 118 small islands. The first Doge/Chief Magistrate was elected in 697 and Venice was a republic, known as La Serenissima (The Most Sublime), until the French took it in 1797 and gave it to the Austrians in exchange for Milan. In 1866 it was incorporated into the new Kingdom of Italy. Venice had great influence and sovereignty over much of the East Mediterranean until the discoveries of the Cape route to the East and the New World led to its decline. But, it remains an important port and manufacturing city and, although struggling against sinking into the Adriatic, with its magnificent architecture, 160 canals and 400 bridges, it draws tourists from all over the world. Nationalism is, however, rife today and in May, 1997, a small group briefly occupied the 325-foot Campanile (Bell Tower) in St Mark's Square. Their objective is to restore the independent republic of La Serenissima.

27   TRIPOLI

Floating mines were still a danger after the war and we passed close to a shell-encrusted horned mine shortly after noon the next day. We, however, had no need to report it to a shore station, as we had already been alerted of its presence by a warning transmitted by the *Sampan* (BKXY).

Our soldier passengers/supernumeraries were all young recruits; fresh out from the UK and going to Libya for training. Their officer was Lieut. May; a congenial man in his late twenties. Mr May sat beside me at the meal table and we soon learned that his favourite topic of conversation was the Army. During a meal, he said, "One thing which the British Army requires of its officers, is that they must be able to do anything that the men have to do. If a man's in the infantry, he must be able to....". And when, at this point, Ernest interrupted by saying, "walk", we all burst out laughing.

When we were nearing Tripoli, Ffoulkes handed me a telegram addressed to the Agent to let them know of our draft and time of arrival. I called the radio station in Tripoli, but, after several fruitless calls, Malta (VPT) offered to take the message. "But shouldn't I be able to raise Tripoli?" I asked. "Could do," replied the operator, "but I haven't heard him since the war"! This was his humorous way of telling me that there was now no radio station in Tripoli!

The sea had been dead calm the whole way, but, early on the morning of Thursday, 6 March and when we were close to the port, a sandstorm blew up and visibility was reduced to about half a mile. Ffoulkes asked for a D/F bearing, but as there was no radio station or beacon available, this was impossible and the navigators had to prowl about slowly until the entrance to the port was found. In addition to reducing visibility, the sandstorm made things very unpleasant. The temperature rose by about 13°C and, because I had neglected to close my portholes, there was sand all over my cabin. And, for those on deck, it was a most unusual experience to have hot sand blown into their faces while at sea.

I stood on deck as we entered the harbour which was full of ships, some of which were fairly large. But it was a sobering fact to find that they were all wartime wrecks and that we were the only vessel capable of movement. I counted nine wrecks, but someone said there were fifteen. Tripoli was an ominously quiet port as we tied up alongside on Thursday afternoon and the Agent boarded with a considerable amount of mail. I received four letters including one from a regular correspondent whose letters never contained much more news than what the weather had been like in Dundee! To our disappointment, no shore leave was permitted due an outbreak of smallpox in the town. We were all vaccinated, but, as it took several days for the vaccinations to become effective, this was of no use to us.

Throughout the discharging, we had ten soldiers on board guarding the ship and as this was more than I ever saw during the war, I considered it to be a way of keeping the young men occupied. We were again in range of the American Forces Network in Europe and I enjoyed listening to the 'Baby Snook's Show' and 'Duffy's Tavern'.

I was unaware that we had carried anything other than vehicles and ammunition until a search party, composed of officers and redcaps, boarded and I was required to accompany them in their search of the ship. A great deal of army clothing and binoculars were missing and they searched even Ffoulkes' quarters, without success. We surmised that the items had been stolen on their way to the ship in Venice, but the search exonerated us and when a few shore passes arrived for those who had to go ashore on business, I had my excuse to see something of Tripoli.

The shops were not as well stocked as those in Italy, but I was able to make a good purchase of a set of stamps bearing the heads of both Hitler and Mussolini. (The rate of exchange was 480 lire to £1.) The Arab quarter was fenced off and out of bounds to the Forces, but, from a distance I could see areas cleared of buildings which had been destroyed in the fighting. My wanderings took me to the harbour wall where a number of Arabs stood in the sunshine watching a ship moving in the harbour. And panic seized me when I realized that it was the *Samnesse*. I had not been aware that she was moving to an outer anchorage and didn't know how to get back on board. But when I went to the office of the British Harbour Master and explained my predicament, he provided a motor launch.

It was only because one our winches had broken down that I was able to visit the town at all. We had been due to sail on Tuesday evening, but owing to parts of the winch being taken ashore for repair, our departure was postponed until Thursday. On Thursday afternoon, however, word came from the engineering workshop that the parts wouldn't be ready until 10am the following morning. As soon as they arrived, we sailed at 10.32 am on Friday, 14 March for Bône, in Algeria.

We were at sea the following afternoon when Tony appeared at the door of my cabin and stood looking at me in a somewhat quizzical fashion before saying, "The transmitter's on the bum again." It was, of course, a serious matter, but, infected by his expression and seeing him waiting for my reaction, I began to laugh and we laughed together uncontrollably before returning to face the reality of the situation. As the power transformer, rewound in Lourenço Marques, had been a previous source of trouble, it was the first thing we looked at and found that it, and a choke associated with it, had burned out.

Postscript: Similar to Eritrea, Libya was a former Italian colony under British control. The Italians had taken possession of Libya, from the Ottoman Turks, in 1911/12 and it was from there that they launched their attack on Egypt a few months after their entry into the war, in 1940. Then, when it looked as if the Italians were about to be defeated by the British and Commonwealth Western Desert Force, Hitler had sent in a force to support them. Tripoli had been the German port of entry and, on 12 February, 1941, it was there that Rommel first set foot on North African soil. Tripoli had been occupied by the Germans until the victorious Eighth Army entered it on 23 January, 1943 and Britain controlled Libya until 24 December, 1951 when, under a Sanusi king, it became the first independent state created by the United Nations. In 1969, a revolution, led by Colonel Qadhafi, resulted in the overthrow of the monarchy. In 2011, however, Qadhafi.was removed by NATO (and subsequently killed) and the country is now governed by the General National Congress with Islam the state religion.

28   BONE AND THE 'LAST LEG'

As I had to deal with port officials, I was up by 6 o'clock on the morning of Sunday, 16 March and stood on deck as we approached the town. On the narrow fertile plain, between the sea and the hills, Bône looked lovely in the clear morning air and, with a pilot on board, we tied up at a quay close to the town centre at 6.44am.

When Alan Curry and I made our first trip into the town in the afternoon, we thought it a very nice place with its wide palm-lined streets rising towards the cork tree covered foothills of the Djebel-Edough. As it was a Sunday, the shops were closed, but the cafés, along the wide main street were open and, in typical French style, the 'pieds-noirs'/Algerian-born French sat at tables outside them enjoying drinks. And, when we found a barbershop open, Alan and I had badly needed haircuts.

As we had neither the wire nor the skill to rewind the transformer, I informed the Agent of this on our arrival. An electrical engineer took it ashore on the Monday morning and we hoped that the repair would be done quickly so as not to delay our departure. But the engineer reported that the transformer had been badly wound in Lourenço Marques and that, due to a shortage of wire, he was unable to repair it. His solution was to replace it with a transformer of a much lower step-up ratio which reduced our transmitting range to only about 100 miles during daylight. To sail in this condition was illegal, but the British Consul issued a permit to allow us to do so.

The *Samtampa* came in during our stay and, Bill Waters, her R/O, paid us a friendly visit. He was not, however, the man who was lost when the ship was driven onto rocks at Sker Point, near Porthcawl, the following month and missed the fate of his successor by a mere quirk of fate. When the ship arrived in Middlesbrough, IMR (International Marine Radio) asked if he would like to remain on her for the short run to South Wales. They did this because South Wales was nearer to Mr Waters' home and he declined the offer only because he had already packed his bags. When I later worked at Portisheadradio, within which Burnhamradio was situated, a colleague showed emotion as he spoke of this disaster and recalled the bravery of the R/O, W.E. Thompson. With death staring him in the face, his last message had been to thank Burnham for their assistance.

During my visits to Algeria in 1943 and 1944, the rate of exchange had been 200 francs to the £1; now it was 480.

Postscript: Bône or Bona took its name from a holy woman called Lella Bona and was, after Algiers and Oran, the third most important port in French Algeria. Its population was 70,000, about half of whom were French. When the French took the town in 1832 they called it Bône, but when Algeria won its independence from France in 1962, it was given the Arabic name Annaba; 'city of the jujube trees'.

I cannot recall what we loaded in Bône, but we sailed at 10.37 am on Wednesday. 19 March and, at long last, were headed for home. And I and the few other Scots on board were particularly happy that we were bound for Glasgow.

We were passing Gibraltar at 7am on Saturday, 22 March and because of our reduced transmitting range, made a point of communicating with the radio station (ZDK) on the 'Rock'. The ship began to roll heavily when we entered the Atlantic. Speed was reduced to only 8.5 knots and, due to the incessant rolling, I slept only fitfully during Saturday and Sunday nights. But, by Monday night the sea was calmer and speed was increased to 9.5 knots. Towards dinnertime on Wednesday, 26 March, when we neared the coast of England, we heard Landsendradio (GLD) calling us (MYMX). The message redirected us to Birkenhead, which delighted everybody but the Scots, and I was destined never to return to a port in Scotland from a foreign voyage.

Visibility was bad when we approached the Mersey the following day so that I was again required to use the direction finder as we headed for the Bar Light Ship. The Lynas pilot provided me with a portable radio-telephony transmitter in order to communicate with Gladstone Dock, but, standing in pouring rain on the bridge, we called the Dock station for nearly three hours before they answered and told us they we were to dock on the PM tide the next day. As I stood calling Gladstone, Ken Crawford said that they could not possibly hear me when I was not speaking into a microphone. This was not a stupid remark. The transmitter had a throat microphone and, similar to Ken, I had never come across one before.

As this was the first time I had approached a homeport as purser, I spent endless hours calculating the wages due to each man. The day of pay-off was crucial to my calculations and I constantly altered the pencilled-in figures on the individual wages sheets as the final day of the voyage was uncertain.

We were at anchor in the Mersey, on Friday, 28 March, when the order was given to proceed into the dock, in Birkenhead. But the anchor fouled on the riverbed. We informed Gladstone of our predicament and they heightened the tension by saying that, if we could not be at the lock gates by such-and-such a time, when the tide had fallen to the level at which they had to be closed, we could not enter. All on board were now anxious as the windlass struggled to raise the anchor. But the deadline passed and the ship remained stuck.

The situation was particularly frustrating to those who lived in the Merseyside area. They had expected to be home that evening, but, within sight of the Liver Birds, we lay in the river throughout Saturday when Liverpool was experiencing the excitement of the Grand National. Everyone participated in the sweepstake which I ran, and, ironically, it was the Mersey pilot who drew the Irish horse Caughoo which, ridden by E. Dempsey, came first at 100 to 1. The pilot was on the bridge with Ffoulkes when I handed him his winnings and said that it had been won by a rank outsider. "Was it? replied the pilot innocently. "He means you", laughed Ffoulkes.

The anchor chain had to be cut and we docked early on Sunday morning. A clerk from the Liverpool Office collected my wages book and, when he informed me that final wages forms were made out by the Office, I dumped all the, thirty-odd, forms, over which I had spent so many anxious hours, into my waste-paper basket. Also, in the morning, I issued travel warrants to the crew. Mrs Ffoulkes passed my door on the way to greet her husband and, shortly after lunch, someone told me that there was a young lady on the quay looking for Tony. This was Tony's girlfriend and I informed her, from the top of the gangway, that Tony had gone to see *her*. It was only afterwards that it occurred to me that I should have invited her on board and regretted that I had not done so. It was a considerable journey to the ship from her home in Liverpool and no doubt she would liked to have seen something of the vessel on which her boyfriend had spent many months.

The Customs cleared the ship in afternoon and I paid [25] 19/8d (98p) duty on the articles I brought into the country. In the evening, Ernest I hired a taxi to take us to Lime Street Station and deposited our gear in the left-luggage

---

[25] Almost all of us had no British currency so that before we arrived, I passed a sheet round asking what each man wanted. This was known as Channel Money and was brought to the ship when she docked. At that time, it was limited to either £2 or one-quarter of the balance of wages due, whichever was the lesser.

office. We then had a late meal in the Tudor Restaurant before returning to the ship by the Birkenhead Ferry.

Mr Stocks, the Company's Radio Superintendent, boarded on Monday morning and I told him about the faults in the transmitter. And in the afternoon the saloon was crowded when the Birkenhead Shipping Master sat at a table and witnessed us signing off the Articles. I paid-off with £35.7.11d, but as my mother had been buying National Savings Certificates for me with my £12 a month allotment, I have saved approximately £150 during the voyage. Mr Bevins, the Bosun, paid-off with the highest balance of £167.8.9 although his monthly salary was only [26]£26 and he had left an allotment of £3 a week to his wife. And next to him came young Mr Jenkins who had already gone from the ship to pay-off at the shipping office in Cardiff. In spite of having his fireman's salary of only [27]£24.10/-, leaving £6 a month to his mother and paying insurance contributions, he had saved £122.18.6d. Fred Crampthorn, the Deck Boy, also demonstrated an ability to handle money. From his meagre salary of [28]£15, and after leaving £2 a month to his mother, he had saved £9.15/-; pretty good for a young lad on his first voyage. Although the names of midshipmen/deck apprentices were recorded on the Articles, they did not sign them as the rest of us did. I cannot recall what Alan and Peter were paid, but, from their small and inadequate pay, they left allotments of £4 and £5 a month respectively.

I was in my cabin when the Bosun appeared at my door. He was angry and, with his wages account in his hand, demanded to know what right I had to deduct Union subscriptions. At the beginning of the voyage, I had been given a sheet from the National Union of Seamen listing the names of all those who had contracted to pay, with each man's signature against his name. When I showed the Bosun the sheet which he had signed, it took the wind out of his sails. Later in the afternoon, Tony and I reported at India Buildings and, on leaving the Office, I transferred my gear to Exchange Street Station. In the evening I went to a cinema before returning to the depressingly silent ship. There were now only a few men on board and as replacement Chinese stewards had put no sheets or blankets on my bunk, I slept under a greatcoat provided by the Mate. This neglect of those remaining on board at the end of a voyage was not

---

[26, 27, 28] These figures include the War Risk Money.

uncommon as it was assumed by the relieving Chief Steward that all who had made the deep-sea voyage in her lived locally and were tucked up in their own beds.

I was wakened early in the morning of Tuesday, 1 April, 1947 by a Glasgow 'standby' engineer and, after breakfast, bade farewell to the few remaining officers before heading for Exchange Street Station and boarding the 9.43am train for Scotland. A number of German prisoners, in their drab POW uniforms, boarded the train at Carstairs and I was in Dundee by 7.30pm. A taxi had me home by about 8 o'clock and, as I had deliberately withheld the news that we were homeward bound, when writing from Bône, my homecoming was the surprise that I meant it to be.

Postscript: Captain Ffoulkes died in 1976; shortly after my family and I had spent a second holiday at his home in Birkenhead. He was devoted to the Methodist Church and, even in his eighties took charge of *old* people on coach trips.

As already mentioned, the *Samnesse* was one of the Liberty Ships supplied to Britain under the wartime Lease-Lend Agreement between Britain and the United States of America. British shipowners managed them on behalf of the Ministry of War Transport and, when the war was over, were given the opportunity to buy them at a reduced price. Holts bought the *Samnesse* and she made only a short trip to Casablanca, before they renamed her *Eumaeus* (GBZJ). She was, subsequently called *Glenshiel* and then *Euryrades* before they sold her in 1961. As the *Marine Bounty*, she, in 1966, ran aground on the coast of China, broke in two, and became a total loss. And, on that final passage, from Chingwangtao to Singapore, she was carrying coal!

29   LEITH NAUTICAL COLLEGE

I had made up my mind to go for my 1st Class PMG and, as Dundee Wireless College had closed, went to Leith Nautical College. I began there on Wednesday, 7 May, 1947 and because it was a Central Institution, and not privately owned as had been the case in Dundee, the fee was only a nominal £5 for as long as it took to upgrade my ticket. Ironically, the fee to sit the exam was exactly double that amount.

The College had three Departments; Navigation, Engineering and Radio. Mr W.A. Fisher was the Principal and Mr Andrew Bogie Head of the Radio Department, with Mr Watson his sole assistant.

The Radio Department consisted of lecture room, Morse room and a room containing the very latest marine equipment. There were two classes - one studying for the 2nd Class PMG and the other for the 1st Class. All the 2nd Class students were ex-servicemen on Government grants to allow them to train for civilian employment. But although the 1st Class students had been in the Merchant Navy during the war, they were not entitled to grants as they already had the lower qualification which was sufficient to obtain a job.

All of the students had interesting stories to tell, but none more so than Bill Walker who had been a prisoner on the *Altmark* after his ship was sunk by the *Admiral Graf Spee*. In defiance of international law, HMS *Cossack* intercepted the *Altmark* in Norwegian territorial waters and brought her prisoners to Leith. This historic event occurred in February, 1940 and being a local boy, of only 16 at the time, Bill made the lead story in the local newspaper.

The exam for the 1st Class PMG extended over three days and was divided into the following sections.

1. Receiving and sending plain language Morse at 25 wpm and code at 20 wpm.
2. Commercial working - in Morse.
3. Electricity and Magnetism - two hour written paper.
4. Wireless Telegraphy - three hour written paper.
5. Questions on regulations by examiner (about 30 minutes).
6. Questions on equipment by examiner - anything up to 3 hours when two students were present.

Of the five of us who sat the exam in November, only one passed. But all succeeded the following March. Failure in one section meant retaking the entire exam and it was some years later before a resit of the Morse test alone was allowed.

We also had to have a knowledge of the world's principal shipping routes and when the student with me was asked how a ship would go from Leith to somewhere on the other side of the Atlantic, he neglected to say how she would get round Scotland. But, when the GPO examiner, Mr Frank Adams, pulled him up on this and he said, "Through the Forth and Clyde Canal", his answer was accepted with a wry smile. The Forth and Clyde Canal had fallen into disuse and, in any case, could never accommodate any vessel large enough to require an R/O.

I generally went home at weekends to see a girl I had met, and fallen for, while on leave and these rail journeys were made at reduced cost by obtaining vouchers from the Radio Officers' Union.

Finding digs turned out to be something of an on-going problem and, when I first went to Leith, a friend of my father put me in touch with Mr and Mrs Buchanan of 7 Rosslyn Crescent, Edinburgh who took me in until I found accommodation. This resulted in me staying in their home for two nights and, although they didn't know me and also provided meals, (Mrs Buchanan even gave me a row for taking one out!) they refused any payment.

Cambridge Gardens consisted of terraced, stone, villas and I moved in with Mr and Mrs Emslie at No.15 the same day I began at College. Mrs Emslie, a fresh-faced stout woman of about forty, was hard of hearing. Her husband was a small, wiry man somewhat older than she was and their other lodger was Jim White, a joiner from Dundee. Mrs Emslie liked to talk and once when she was gabbing away while we were anxious for our tea, I said, "Go and get our tea ready" in a low voice which she wasn't meant to hear. She did, however, know that I had spoken, but, when appealed to, Jim insisted that I hadn't said anything. Jim was a bit of a card and when he spoke disparagingly of the police entrance exam, he said, "All they ask you are questions like how many petals are on a daisy" - a question which would have floored all applicants!

When Mrs Emslie announced that they were going for a fortnight's holiday in June, she said that we would have to have our tea elsewhere as she was having a perm. Mrs Lord, in Wellington Place agreed to provide my meals during the fortnight, but Mrs Emslie demanded full normal payment just the same. I didn't stay long with the Emslies after that and, as I found other digs for the fortnight, I didn't take up Mrs Lord's offer. When I was absolutely stuck for a place to spend the night of 5 January, 1948, Mrs Lord put me up on the settee in her living room. I was absolutely freezing, but for supper, *bed* and breakfast, she charged me only 2/6d (12½p).

Looking for a place to stay when the Emslies were on holiday, I was about to pull one of the brass knobs at the entrance to a tenement at Crighton Place in Leith Walk when a man addressed me from behind. I turned to find that we had travelled on a train to Dundee together. He was with his wife and when I explained the situation, they said I could spend the fortnight with them.

My benefactors were Jim and Margaret Johnstone who lived in the tenement at 46 Dalmeny Street and we became friends. As they had only two bedrooms, Margaret moved in with their young daughter, Myrtle, and I slept with Jim. They were active members of South Leith Baptist Church and through them I met others who became friends. Margaret suffered from both alopecia and bad eyesight, but she and Jim always made me welcome at their home and, on the odd evening, Jim would call at my digs to persuade me to desert my studies and go out for the evening. When Jim's brother was in the Glasgow Infirmary, he wrote asking Baptist friends if he could stay with them for the weekend of 24/25 January, 1948 and because he had mentioned me in the letter, I too was invited. This resulted in a new friendship for me and, on future visits to Glasgow, I was made just as welcome at the home of the Crabbs in Glasgow as I was at the Johnstone's.

Due to the summer recess, it was Monday, 25 August, before I moved into the tenement home of Mr and Mrs Brown at 19 Constitution Street which was just below the foot of Leith Walk and nearer the College. Although in a less affluent area, the digs were much better as I was treated like a member of the family. Mrs Brown was a big woman from Buckhaven in Fife while her husband, although quiet and small, had been in the trenches of France during the Great War when only sixteen. The Brown's had a son, David, of about nine, and William, about a year old. I had my meals with them and, after tea, David always wanted me to stay to listen to Dick Barton on the radio. David was a fine boy with red hair like his Dad, a carter with the railway, based at the Leith Depot. Every day David asked his Dad what he had been driving. Was it a horse and cart or a Scammell?

Eric had been called up for National Service on 5 June and, after a few weeks with the Black Watch at Queens Barracks in Perth, was sent to Barnard Castle in Yorkshire to train as a Tech. Ack. (Technical Assistant) in the Royal Artillery. On his way home on leave, on Friday, 12 September, he broke his journey to see me. Mrs Brown gave him tea and breakfast and he slept with me. And I don't think she charged him anything.

A young cheerful soldier stayed at Mrs Brown's for a brief period. While serving in Italy, he had been wounded in the eyes due to inaccurate fire from our own guns. It was thought at first that he would be totally blind, but, after he had lain for weeks with both eyes bandaged, the surgeons succeeded in saving one eye. He therefore wore a glass one and startled me by taking in out to show it to me.

On the evening of 21 October, my father, who was in Edinburgh on business, paid an unexpected visit. When he saw that the walls over my bed were decorated with pictures of railway engines secured by 1" nails, he couldn't get over it and said, "I'll better not tell your mother about this." The room had, of course, been David's and when I returned from Dundee one Sunday evening when I was not expected until Monday, an embarrassed Mrs Brown hastily removed him from my bed. But I couldn't care less about the decoration. I had a small table to work on and a small electric fire to keep me warm - all for about thirty bob a week. Almost everyone listened to the radio programme 'Forces Favourites' at dinner/lunch time on Sundays. My room looked out towards the back of tenements in Great Junction Street and I have a memory of hearing the recording of Frank Sinatra singing 'Time After Time' issuing from the open window of a house.

It came as a blow, therefore, when Mrs Brown told me that she had to dispense with boarders as she was pregnant. It was again a case of searching for new digs and, due to the Christmas recess, it was 8 January, 1948 before I got fixed up with another Mrs Brown. This was in the tenement at 4 Admiralty Street, about five minutes walk from the College, and I moved in on Monday the 12th.

The winter of 1947/48 was a severe one and so cold that I invested in heavy underwear. I had to study in the kitchen/living room as my room, even after I obtained a small electric fire on paying an extra five bob (25p), was perishing. It was in fact the sitting room and I went to my bed-settee with more clothes on than I wore during the day. I also piled everything I could on the bed - antimacassars and even a rug - but still froze. Another problem was the social life which went on in the kitchen and which made study almost impossible. On my very first evening, there were visitors in so that I went to the Sailors' Home to study. There was another boarder called Charlie Thompson and, on my second night, he, the Browns and another woman, played cards with the radio on. It was an impossible situation and, on Saturday, I gave Mrs Brown £2 and told her I was leaving because of the cold. Before the Browns went out the following evening, their eight-year-old son, Jim, was put to bed and Charlie and I were left to act as baby sitters.

I moved into the centrally heated Sailors' Home, in Tower Place, on Monday. I had temporarily stayed there the previous August, before going to the first Mrs Brown's, when, as all the officers' rooms were taken, I had occupied a room in the midst of a group of Finnish sailors. There were about twenty-four rooms in the officers' section and I now had one of them. All the others were allocated to students at the College and, apart from one tall blond man from Shetland studying navigation, all were studying radio. The rooms, separated only by partitions, were narrow and spartan, without washhand basins. But they were adequate and there was an officers' dining room and a lounge, both overlooking the dock. The dining room was spacious and pleasant while the lounge was palatial with tables, leather-bound easy chairs and pictures of sailing ships on the walls. And, as we were all students, that was where we studied. The name 'Sailors' Home' may sound unattractive, but it was warm, comfortable and friendly and dances were held on Wednesday evenings.

As food rationing was still in operation, we gave our coupons to Mr MacDonald, a former Chief Steward who was the officer-in-charge. But as the amount of food served was inadequate and we did not get the number of eggs to which we were entitled, I decided to do something about it. After consulting the others, I wrote a letter of complaint to the British Sailors' Society in Glasgow, on Wednesday 3 March, and got them to append their signatures below mine.

When we went in for lunch on Friday, all our plates were so piled up that the boys were looking across at me and smiling. Nothing had been said, but what a difference! During the evening, however, a minion entered the lounge and rudely said, "The boss wants to see you, you and you." The others immediately rose to the summons, but I said, "Hold on a minute, if he wants to see us he can come here." With some trepidation, they sat down again and he did. But the discussion was friendly and, as he promised us more scran, the crisis was over.

It was Monday, 5 April, 1948 when I 'phoned the College from the red kiosk near my house in Dundee to find out the result of the exam. And on learning that I'd passed, I boarded the 2.43pm train to Edinburgh to commence the Radar Observers' Course which had started that same day.

The other students on the fortnight course were navigating officers and all but one were Norwegian Masters of Salvesen's whale catchers. But, knowing my profession, Mr Dickson, the instructor, supplied me with more detailed information about radar in general and the Type 268 set which we used. I now wonder if I were the only radio officer to qualify for the Radar Observers' Certificate. Merchant ships were only beginning to have radar and a maintenance course was about to be introduced at the College for radio officers. Mr Bogie tried to get us to take it, but, as it extended over a period of three or four months and we were paying our own way, no-one was interested.

Incidentally, my acquisition on a 1st Class PMG was only a matter of pride as Holts didn't care what certificate you had as long as you could do the purser's work. It was mandatory that the R/O-in-charge on Class I passenger vessels held a 1st Class, but none of Alfred Holt's ships came into this category. They made no extra payment for having the higher award and the majority of their R/Os had only a 2nd Class PMG. Similarly, the Radar Observers' Certificate was of no interest to them and, when I eventually served on a ship with radar, it was the mates who operated it and an electrician, who knew little or nothing about it, was responsible for its maintenance.

On Tuesday, 13 April, 1948, I went up to Dalmeny Street to bid farewell to the Johnstones who were to remain friends for several years to come.

I left with a great affection for Leith where I had met much kindness and where, on the very day I left the College with my brand new 1st Class PMG in my pocket, I got a friendly wave from Mr Brown who happened to be passing with his horse and cart.

On informing Holts that I was again ready for duty, I received the following telegram in the early evening of Friday 23 April. "REPORT MARINE SUPERINTENDENT GLASGOW MON 26TH COAST RELIEF DUTIES = ODYSSEY". And now holding the top qualification, it was with enthusiasm that I returned to sea after a year's absence.

Other seafaring books by Ian M. Malcolm

LIFE ON BOARD A WARTIME LIBERTY SHIP (print and ebook formats, published by Amberley)

Describes the author's wartime experiences as the 3rd Radio Officer of the Liberty Ships *Samite* and *Samforth*.

BACK TO SEA (print and ebook formats, published by Moira Brown)

A voyage to the Far East on the 1911-built *Atreus*, which carries pilgrims to Jeddah on her homeward passage. The author then attends the Lifeboat School in Liverpool and stands by the 1928-built *Eurybates* in Belfast before making his first two voyages on Glen Line's *Glengarry*.

VIA SUEZ (print and ebook formats, published by Moira Brown)

The author makes two more voyages on the *Glengarry* before requesting a voyage to Australia prior to swallowing the anchor. He then coasts the *Glengarry*, *Elpenor/Glenfinlas*, *Helenus*, *Patroclus*, *Medon* and *Clytoneus* after which he is told that his request has been granted. (Photographs/illustrations.)

LAST VOYAGE AND BEYOND (print and ebook formats, published by Moira Brown)

The Australian part of the voyage, on *Deucalion* (built in 1920 as the *Glenogle*) proves enjoyable, but is followed by a trip round Indonesian islands, loading copra, which, although a most interesting experience, is not. On returning home, the author spends two unhappy years in a Dundee office after which he works at GPO Coast Stations for three years, before resigning to train as a teacher in Edinburgh.

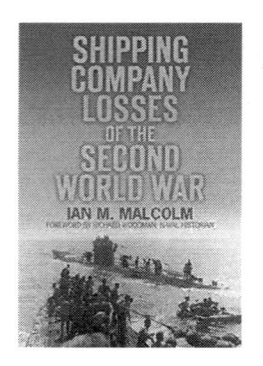

SHIPPING COMPANY LOSSES OF THE SECOND WORLD WAR (print and ebook formats, published by the History Press)

Describes the losses suffered by 53 companies in detail; giving masters' names, where bound, convoy numbers, positions when sunk, casualties and enemy involved.

LETTERS FROM A RADIO OFFICER (print and ebook formats, published by Moira Brown)

Letters sent to the author from a former shipmate who, from 1951 till 1963, served with Brocklebank, Marconi, Redifon (ashore and afloat), the Crown Agents, Clan Line, the Royal Fleet Auxiliary (RFA), Ferranti (in Edinburgh), and Marconi again before settling for a shore job in London.

DANGEROUS SEAS (print and ebook formats, published by Moira Brown)

Four book collection – *Dangerous Voyaging, Dangerous Voyaging 2, Fortunes of War* and *Mined Coasts*.

The reader will be left in no doubt of the sacrifices made by the men, and also a few women, of the wartime Merchant Navy.

Printed in Great Britain
by Amazon